P9-CQG-080

The

Home Team

The

Home Team

Spiritual Practices for a Winning Family

Nate Adams

Revell
Grand Rapids, Michigan

© 2004 by Nate Adams

Published by Fleming H. Revell
a division of Baker Publishing Group
P.O. Box 6287, Grand Rapids, MI 49516-6287
www.bakerbooks.com

Printed in the United States of America

All rights reserved. No part of this publication may be reproduced, stored in a retrieval system, or transmitted in any form or by any means—for example, electronic, photocopy, recording—without the prior written permission of the publisher. The only exception is brief quotations in printed reviews.

Library of Congress Cataloging-in-Publication Data
Adams, Nate.
    The home team : spiritual practices for a winning family / Nate Adams.
        p.   cm.
    Includes bibliographical references.
    ISBN 0-8007-5928-1 (pbk.)
    1. Family—Religious life. I. Title
BV4526.3.A33 2004
249—dc22   2004003799

Unless otherwise indicated, Scripture is taken from the *Holy Bible*, New Living Translation, copyright © 1996. Used by permission of Tyndale House Publishers, Inc., Wheaton, Illinois 60189. All rights reserved.

Scripture marked NIV is taken from the HOLY BIBLE, NEW INTERNATIONAL VERSION®. NIV®. Copyright © 1973, 1978, 1984 by International Bible Society. Used by permission of Zondervan. All rights reserved.

To my wife, Beth,
and our three terrific sons,
Caleb, Noah, and Ethan.
Thanks, God, for the privilege of practicing life
with such a great home team.

Contents

Introduction   9

1. Circling the Wagons   13
   The Practice of Reading Together
2. Telling the Stories   33
   The Practice of Eating Together
3. Making the List   47
   The Practice of Playing Together
4. Finding the Fun   63
   The Practice of Working Together
5. Following the Leader   79
   The Practice of Worshiping Together
6. Going the Distance   97
   The Practice of Traveling Together
7. Sharing the Pain   115
   The Practice of Hurting Together
8. Boarding the Bus   131
   The Practice of Changing Together

Contents

9. Trading the Seat   149
   The Practice of Fighting Together

10. Finding the Future   165
    The Practice of Dreaming Together

11. Ringing the Bell   183
    The Practice of Serving Together

12. Preparing the Path   201
    The Practice of Praying Together

Notes 219

Introduction

There are lots of good books today about raising a Christian family. Psychologists and other family experts have helped us immensely with their research, insights, and suggested techniques. Many have probed the various developmental stages, personality types, and cultural pressures that influence today's families.

This book is a little different. It doesn't seek to analyze families from the inside so much as to observe their positive habits from the outside. I have started with this simple question: What does a healthy Christian family look like? The image that best answers that question for me is a team, a "home team," that consistently engages in certain effective practices. Let me illustrate.

When I played high school basketball, our team's dream was to have a winning season and go to the state championship. Unfortunately, throughout the season our opponents consistently scored more points than we did, and the first game of our regional tournament was no exception. So we did get to go to the state championship but as spectators instead of participants. Instead of a winning team on a mission, we became a wannabe team in a Mazda, driving down to the state capital to watch the real winning teams pursue our dream.

The guys on our team did love the game though. So much so that we attended not only every game in the championship tournament but also every practice session. Because the games were held in the university's huge arena, each of the "elite eight" teams was granted some practice time under the big dome. Those practices were open to the public, and my teammates and I found we could get much better seats at the practice sessions than we could at the games.

We actually learned even more about what makes a winning team by watching those practices than we did by watching the games. These winning teams ran drills we had never seen before—and at a level of intensity and commitment we had never experienced in our games, let alone our practices. Their simple warm-up drills were more purposeful than ours. Their shooting drills were more efficient than ours. Their conditioning drills were more rigorous, and their scrimmages were more focused. In short, we concluded that these teams were winners because of their practices. What we saw on the court at game time was a direct result of what we saw behind the scenes.

Winning families are home teams that have effective practices. If we were to sit in the bleachers of their home courts and observe their daily activities and routines, we would gain a great deal of insight into what makes them winners in life.

As I've observed happy, healthy, winning families over the years, I've counted twelve "practices" they seem to perform with teamwork and dedication. Those practices are the subject of this book. My hope is that by understanding and imitating these practices, many other families will become winning home teams as they play the game of life together.

Each chapter starts with an experience from my own home team that illustrates the importance of a particular practice. Then the practice is described and anchored to a key passage from the Bible that illustrates how that practice is God's idea. Each chapter then closes with a handful of tips to help our families with that practice and three practical suggestions for starting or strengthening that practice in our own homes.

In addition, more than seventy-five Scripture passages are sprinkled throughout these twelve practices. In fact, each tip is much more than a human observation about a human family. It's a principle for implementing a practice found in God's Word.

Today millions of Christian parents are actively engaged in the life lab of raising children and seeking to provide a Christian home life. Each family is a home team and has a home-court advantage that comes from God's presence and power. The reality is that most of us parents know far more than we are doing. We simply need help moving the desires of our hearts and the knowledge in our heads to the disciplines of our homes.

If we observe more of these simple practices and introduce them to our own home teams, I believe our families will become stronger and have more consistent victories over our cultural and spiritual opponents. Beginning to imitate and embrace these practices will help us take immediate steps to steer our hectic homes toward a more Christ-like center.

Your family is a home team with winning potential. You have a home-court advantage and a great Coach. Practice well.

Teach your children to choose the right path, and when they are older, they will remain upon it.

Proverbs 22:6

1

Circling the Wagons

The Practice of Reading Together

Today almost any teacher, educator, or child psychologist will tell you that reading is fundamental to a child's development and success in life and that parents should read to their children often.

But for a family seeking to keep Christ at the center of their home, the benefits of reading together can be so much more than educational. Gathering to read out loud together can be to today's family what "circling the wagons" was to early pioneer families. It can create a circle of safety, a circle of fellowship and love, and a circle of rest from the busy journey of life. When the Bible and devotional books are chosen as the reading material, and group prayer is chosen as the response, the circle can also become a circle of faith. There's no better reason to circle the wagons than to infuse your family with God's Word.

Of course, reading together can take on different forms during various stages of a family's life. Our family includes three boys, five if you count the dog and me. When our two older boys were toddlers, my wife, Beth, would coax them to bed with the promise of a quick bedtime story, and I would promptly offer them an action-packed trip to bed by flying them through the air like fighter planes. Sometimes I would hold them upside down by their feet so they could "walk on the ceiling" all the way to bed. Other times I would bounce them like jet-powered pogo sticks until they landed, queasy and giggling, on their beds.

So you see, for us the minutes before bedtime have always consisted of Beth trying to calm the kids down and me trying to rile them up. Eventually our wild bedtime habits led Beth to give me an ultimatum. "OK, you've got them all juiced up. Now *you* try to read them a story."

Now, early on we started reading our kids a great little Bible storybook that surveyed the Bible's main events from creation to revelation. It had colorful, cartoonlike illustrations and easy-to-read sentences. The more we read it to them, the more familiar the simply worded stories became to all of us. Before long I could recite from memory most of the stories in the book. And so could the boys.

So when Beth challenged me to read our wound-up sons a bedtime Bible story, I simply turned the Bible stories into activities. The unwritten scripts would have read something like this:

Jonah and the Great Fish—"God told Jonah to go to Nineveh, but Jonah got on a boat and went the other way [place child on his or her knees, facing away from you, and start rocking child back and forth]. And God sent a big storm [rock child more violently], and the waves came [rock child like a bucking bronco], and the wind blew [blow hard on back of child's neck]. And the sailors said, 'Throw Jonah overboard!' [roll child gently onto the floor]. Then God sent a great big fish to swallow Jonah up [pursue child and scoop him back up in your arms]. And after three days in the belly of the fish [hold your nose, make a face, and say, 'Shoo-wee!'], the fish spit Jonah up on dry land [roll child back onto the floor]. And Jonah got up [child gets up] and went to Nineveh [child walks away], and told the people about God—like he should have in the first place!"

Baby Moses—"The big king called Pharaoh didn't like God's people, even though they were his slaves, and Pharaoh told his soldiers to kill all the baby boys [walk like an Egyptian and then cross your arms and look like a mean pharaoh making a command]. So baby Moses's mother placed him in a basket and hid him in the weeds by the river [scoop up child, carry him behind a chair, and hide him]. When Pharaoh's daughter came down to the river, she found Moses and scooped him up [scoop child up in your arms]. 'Oh, what a beautiful baby!' she cried. [Shriek this line in your shrillest New York accent. I always tried to imitate the nasal whine of Fran Drescher, who played the leading role in TV's *The Nanny*.] 'I just love this beautiful baby!' [Repeat this line over and over, kissing and tickling the child all over.] Moses's sister, Miriam, who had been hiding and watching, stepped forward and said, 'Would you like us to babysit for you?' And so God not only saved Moses but let him stay with his real family while he grew up as a prince [place some kind of crown on child]. That prince would one day lead his people from slavery to a special land God promised them."

The Good Samaritan, or *Robbers*, as our boys came to call it. (This one is great with two or more children. Before beginning, let one or two of the kids hide "down the road" somewhere as the robbers.)—"A man was traveling from Jerusalem down to Jericho. [One child starts walking—with much fear and trepidation and usually giggling—toward where the robbers are hiding.] On the way he ran into some robbers [the robbers jump out of hiding and gently mug the traveler]. And they jumped on him, and they beat him, and they knocked him out [act out the motions while actually tickling and scuffling with the traveler], and they left him for dead with his underwear showing. [As the 'mugging' is completed, tug on the pajamas or shorts of the traveler to expose the child's underwear. To this day our kids think this is hilarious. We started with 'diaper showing' and graduated to 'underwear showing' as they got older.] And a man that worked at the church came by, but did *he* stop and help him? [The children answer, 'No!'] And another man that worked at the church came by, but did *he* stop and help him? [Again the children answer, 'No!'] And then a Samaritan man came by. Did *he* stop to help him? [The children reply, 'Yes!' and while the traveler lays there with his tongue hanging out as if he were dead, another child pretends to bandage up the traveler and help him to his feet.] And the Samaritan man took him to the next town and gave the hotel manager some money [give the child coins to use as a prop] and said, 'Give him whatever he needs.' And that's why we call this man the 'Good Samaritan.'"

Those are just three examples of the Bible stories we made into short, do-it-yourself dramas during a time when our kids were ripe for listening and learning in that way. We eventually had dozens of these in our repertoire. Every time we added another creative action of some kind, that detail became a part of the story from that moment on. When David chose five smooth stones to battle Goliath, one boy got to lie on the floor and wiggle as the babbling brook. When Samson was chained between the two "pillars" of Dad's legs, another boy got to play the roof that caved in on him when he regained his strength. And when Naaman had to dip himself in the Jordan River seven times to be cured of his leprosy, I accidentally dropped our youngest son on his head. To this day our boys probably picture Naaman being dipped seven times in the Jordan River—by his ankles.

And you must love the LORD your God with all your heart,
all your soul, and all your strength. And you must commit
yourselves wholeheartedly to these commands I am giving
you today. Repeat them again and again to your children.
Talk about them when you are at home and when you are
away on a journey, when you are lying down and when you
are getting up again.

Deuteronomy 6:5–7

Of all the practices our family has discovered that invite
Christ into a home, the practice of reading together—and
specifically reading the Bible together in relevant and
age-appropriate ways—is among the most powerful. That
focused time of looking to God can energize the spiritual
lives of our families, because it's like plugging in directly to
God for information, perspective, comfort, and wisdom. It's
almost like we're all running on battery power throughout
the day, then just as our spiritual energy dims, we gather
around God's power strip to plug in and recharge for the
next round of daily life.

Our family's experience with Bible storybooks and action
Bible stories showed that it's never too early to start the
practice of reading the Bible to kids. We've also discovered
that it's never too late to adapt the practice of reading the
Bible together to the needs of our unique family. After a
couple of years or more of action Bible stories at our house,
a job change required that we face the prospect of moving
to another part of the country. We knew this would be a
huge adjustment, not only for Beth and me, but also for
our sons who were then eight, seven, and three. One of the
main ways we chose to process that big life change was
to graduate from our action Bible stories to a prebedtime
family devotion time. I was amazed at how ready our young
children were to look to God every evening to help us with

17

that big transition. So that's when we began a focused time of reading and praying each evening before bed.

The practice of a regular evening devotion time has been part of our family life ever since then, and it continues to strengthen and unify our family in ways I wouldn't have imagined. Through serious family illnesses, through the death of a grandfather and a teacher, through transitions from elementary school to middle school to high school, through disappointments at school and work, through major decisions and minor distractions, through winter blahs and summer vacations, our family devotion time has become a sort of spiritual "circle the wagons" time. It's when we consistently remind ourselves that God is in charge, that his Word is unchanging and true, that we love each other no matter what, and that we will gather like this again tomorrow and face whatever challenges life brings us—together as a family.

Have you discovered the power of a consistent Bible reading and devotional time with your family? Here are some things we've discovered that can make a time like that most meaningful and effective.

Helping Your Family Practice Reading and Praying Together as a Home Team

1. Find the Right Book or Devotional Resource

Tie them to your hands as a reminder, and wear them on your forehead. Write them on the doorposts of your house and on your gates.

Deuteronomy 6:8–9

Even before books were available to Christian families, God encouraged parents to use memory aids and reminders to help them keep God's Word in the forefront of family life. The simply worded Bible storybooks and beginner Bibles we used for our family's initial action Bible stories are one example of an age-appropriate tool that helped us deliver God's Word to our young children.

Of course, as our children get older, the tools we use need to change to adapt to their stages of life. Today there are some very good family devotional books that usually start with a fictional story or situation of some kind and then point to a solution or advice from the Bible. We've also used video clips, current news happenings, or events from a family member's day as the basis for launching into God's Word.

During one vacation at the beach, we did each night's devotion on water passages in the Bible—What was it like to walk on water? What was it like to watch Jesus calm a storm out in a boat? What was it like for Paul to be ship-wrecked? How amazing is it that God created the oceans? On a vacation to the mountains, we did devotions on the mountains of the Bible—Moses climbing the mountain to get the Ten Commandments, what it was like for Noah's ark to come to rest on a mountain, the ways David talked about mountains in the Psalms, and so forth. In each case, we were able to build on that day's experiences and activate our imaginations to help us illustrate the truths of God's Word.

A couple of years before our family's big move to another state, I had written a youth devotional book entitled *Energizers—Light Devotions to Keep Your Faith Growing* that used a lot of my personal experiences of growing up to illustrate biblical truth. When Beth and I decided to start a regular sit-down devotional time with our family, we began with that book simply because it was handy. Even though it was written primarily for a teen audience, our young kids were intrigued with their dad's childhood and teen experiences. That experience taught me the lesson that, while it's important for the right tool to be age-appropriate, it's even more important that the tool capture the personal interest and imagination of the family. With a little creativity, a scene from one of your children's favorite movies or even one of their favorite toys (or yours!) can become a personalized springboard into a principle from the Bible.

In the case of my teen devotional book, the hook was the fact that my kids recognized real people and places in the stories. For the weeks leading up to our move and several weeks afterward, we read those devotions and Bible passages, and our children recognized some of the many changes their dad had been through in his life. Finding the right, personally relevant tool gave us a gateway to God's perspective that helped our family through that stressful time.

What is the right tool for your family? Experimentation may be the best way to find out, and mixing in something new from time to time can keep family devotional times fresh. But we've discovered that finding a good devotional book is like finding spiritual gold, because that kind of tool can give you a consistent resource to rely on, even when you're not feeling especially creative or motivated.

2. Find the Right Time

> The apostles returned to Jesus from their ministry tour and told him all they had done and what they had taught. Then Jesus said, "Let's get away from the crowds for a while and rest." There were so many people coming and going that Jesus and his apostles didn't even have time to eat. They left by boat for a quieter spot.
>
> Mark 6:30–32

Jesus knew the importance of finding "huddle" times with his family of disciples that were separate from the crowds and pressures of daily life. And finding the

20

right time to set aside for reading together and family devotion is critical to success in this habit. With work, school, and home schedules, there usually aren't that many options to choose from. Morning or evening or perhaps during a mealtime are the main times families can be together. For our family, the time right before the bedtime of the youngest child has proven to be the most effective. Mornings are often pretty frantic, and it's often all anyone can do to carve out a few minutes for personal devotions. And we try to use mealtimes for a different practice that is discussed in chapter 2.

Having our family devotion time right before bedtime helps us observe the practice with more regularity and gives us a chance to send our children to bed with thoughts of God and the security of our family fresh on their minds. It also lets us rehash the day and look ahead to tomorrow with prayer and mental and spiritual preparation.

The important thing is to choose the time our families can observe with the greatest consistency. If Mom works second shift, then right before bedtime probably won't work. If Dad commutes several miles to work, then lunchtime is obviously out.

Some families may be in the situation where Mom or Dad travels during the week or can't be there at a regular time each day for some other reason. When I'm traveling for my job, Beth and the boys do devotions without me, and I often schedule my phone call home around that time. That's much better than breaking the habit until I get home or having family devotions only two or three times a week.

In our experience, the practice of reading the Bible together is most effective as a daily habit. That doesn't mean we succeed at having devotions 365 days a year. In fact, I'd caution against becoming so strict with this habit that you insist on having devotions together no matter what.

There are times when we simply need to say, "Not tonight" or "Let's just pray together and get to bed—we've let it get too late."

Finding a daily time to process life with God is well worth it.

But I'd also say that the weeks when we find the discipline to sit and read the Bible and pray together on at least five or six nights are the weeks when we're healthiest and happiest as a family. The Bible has a lot to say about the daily nature of life and about God's daily, moment-by-moment provision. Finding a daily time to process life with God is well worth it.

3. Make It Fun

> They said to each other, "Didn't our hearts feel strangely warm as he talked with us on the road and explained the Scriptures to us?"
>
> Luke 24:32

I love this description of how the disciples on the road to Emmaus felt after they had been with the risen Lord Jesus. And it's a great goal for times of family devotion—that our family members' hearts would feel strangely warm as a result of talking together and having Scripture explained.

Those moments seem to come from being together, learning together, and laughing together. With the busy and scattered schedules most families have, there aren't many times during the week when all members are together and focused on each other. And when we combine that rare moment with a genuine learning experience from God's Word—and mix in a little fun and laughter—we can create moments that will warm hearts both now and for years to come.

For our family, devotions usually begin with a sort of call to worship—"Time for devotions!" And even the assembly time is usually lighthearted—"Who has the book?" "I read last night. You read tonight." "Why does he always get to sit there?" One rule we have is that we can't hold a toy or stuffed animal, another book, or anything that might distract us from the devotion time. That sometimes leads to search and seizure, tickling, or other fun activities.

Even though family members may occasionally protest the summons, the reality is that even this gathering time is an opportunity to reinforce several important truths. We're a family. We're seeking to be a Christian family. It's important that everyone be together for these few minutes. Being a family is ultimately more important than whatever we're doing right now. And yes, sometimes this is even fun.

Some of the fun moments our family has shared during family devotions have stuck with us for years. That line from the "Robbers" (Good Samaritan) story still brings an immediate smile to all our faces—"And they left him for dead with his underwear showing." But interestingly, our kids can also remember that the traveler was going from Jerusalem down to Jericho, because that was always the opening line of the story. And they can remember that the men we would have expected to stop and help the man didn't but that the man who was presumed to be bad ended up being good. In other words, they can remember many important details of that Bible story because they heard it over and over again waiting for their favorite line—"And he left him for dead with his underwear showing."

Often the fun times in family devotions can come spontaneously, during a discussion question or group activity. Go around in a circle and have every family member share his or her answer to a particular question—for example, When do you find it hardest to forgive? or, What was your earliest impression of God? You'll be surprised at some of the humorous responses you receive, even to seemingly serious questions.

There are many ways to add fun to learning, whether it's through one-liners, object lessons, video clips, or an interesting, lighthearted devotion book. The important thing is to explain Scripture in a way that warms the heart.

4. Keep It Simple

Dear brothers and sisters, when I first came to you I didn't use lofty words and brilliant ideas to tell you God's message.

1 Corinthians 2:1

Someone once said, "There's no such thing as a bad short sermon," and the same is true of these spiritual focus times with our families. The more fun and interesting a family devotion can be, the better, but it's also important to keep these times relatively simple. A consistent, uncomplicated time is much more valuable than an elaborate presentation that happens only occasionally. And let me say it again—a good family devotional book can really help by giving us a simple routine to follow without having to reinvent the wheel each time we sit down together.

Paul makes it clear in 1 Corinthians 2:1 that there is power and effectiveness in the simple truths of God's Word when they are presented without pretense or fanfare. He goes on to say in verse 5 of that chapter, "I did this so that you might trust the power of God rather than human wisdom." Because God's Spirit inspires his Word and inhabits our hearts, and because he promises that his Word will accomplish its purpose (Isa. 55:11), we can have a great deal of confidence in even the most basic family devotion time.

Many times Beth and I have said quietly to one another, "Are we doing devotions tonight?" Usually it's when all the work isn't quite done or when one or more of the kids has been especially grumpy. That's when one of us often offers a compromise: "Why don't we just have a quick prayer time and get them off to bed?" But the surprising thing is that once we've made the call ("Time for devotions!") and set aside whatever we were doing, we often find that we have time to read God's Word, read a devotional thought from a book, and share prayer requests and prayer after all.

Keeping it simple makes it easier to decide to try to do devotions together, however brief. And that decision allows your family to embrace for one more day the power of God that comes from reading his Word together.

5. Be Illustrative and Interactive—Use Stories, Questions, and Quizzes

Jesus asked, "How can I describe the Kingdom of God? What story should I use to illustrate it? It is like a tiny mustard seed. Though this is one of the smallest of seeds, it grows to become one of the largest of plants, with long branches where birds can come and find shelter."

He used many such stories and illustrations to teach the people as much as they were able to understand. In fact, in his public teaching he taught only with parables, but afterward when he was alone with his disciples, he explained the meaning to them.

Mark 4:30–34

It encourages me to hear Jesus ask, "How can I describe the Kingdom of God?" In a way, that's the challenge we face with our children, especially when they're at different ages and stages of life. How do we explain the kingdom of God and its spiritual truths in ways that are practical and relevant every day?

The Bible says Jesus used stories, illustrations, and parables, and then explained to his disciples what they meant. And that's what the most effective family devotions are—simple stories and examples that you can put alongside spiritual truths to help explain them.

25

Our family has also found it effective to be not only illustrative but interactive. After we had been reading from a particular devotional book for a while, I noticed that I didn't always seem to have our kids' full attention. So I started informing them at the start of the devotion that there would be a quiz at the end. I was amazed at how well they listened after that! There was a sort of peer pressure to not miss a question, especially not one to which a brother knew the answer.

The quiz soon became a standard part of our evening devotion routine for several reasons. It motivated everyone to listen more closely. It also allowed us to test our sons' comprehension of both the story and the spiritual principles illustrated in it. And it gave us a way to customize the devotions for the different ages and developmental stages of our kids. Five years separate our oldest and youngest, and they could hear the same devotional reading and come away with different levels of observation and insight. So for Ethan, our youngest, I might ask, "What was Barry's best friend's name in this story?" while for Noah, our middle son, I might ask, "Why do you think Barry didn't want to do what his friend asked?" When I quizzed Caleb, our oldest son, I might ask, "How does this Bible verse help us decide what to do if we're ever in a situation like Barry was?"

Another great benefit of quizzes during devotions is that the kids can learn from one another. In fact, they often learn more from one another than from just listening to a parent read. The more Ethan hears Noah answer "why" questions, the more he understands about complex things like underlying motives. And the more Noah hears Caleb apply a principle to a life event, the more he understands how to do the same. The fun part is that Ethan may actually remember more details from a devotional story than his older brothers because they're focusing more on meaning and application. So the whole family has a better grasp of the devotion's content and meaning, as the quiz facilitates an effective summary.

Over time we try to make sure all the kids gradually learn to identify what they have come to call "the point," the main scriptural truth or principle behind the devotion. Often that's the toughest question on the quiz, and when they hit it they often stall for time by asking, "This is 'the point' isn't it?" And while the quiz is also designed for listening and comprehension and retention, its main benefit is that it lets us ask, "Do you get it? Do you see what God's saying here?"

> **That's what the most effective family devotions are—simple stories and examples that you can put alongside spiritual truths to help explain them.**

The more familiar our families get with stories, illustrations, questions, and quizzes, the more capable each member will be of leading the devotion times. And that's very, very rewarding. When one of our kids is leading the devotion times, the others (including us parents!) are doubly intent on doing well on the quiz and on making sure they get "the point."

Watching our kids begin to take turns leading family devotion times as they mature is one of the great joys of this spiritual practice. It can give us an advance glimpse of the day when they will continue this wonderful, powerful practice with their own families.

6. Adapt and Evolve to Meet the Needs of Children at Different Ages

Dear brothers and sisters, when I was with you I couldn't talk to you as I would to mature Christians. I had to talk as though you belonged to this world or as though you were infants in the Christian life.

1 Corinthians 3:1

From children's Bible stories to action Bible stories to family devotional books to youth devotional books—different tools can be useful at different stages in our families' lives. And the quiz technique is one example of how the same devotional story can be brought to different levels of application for children of different ages. The important principle at work here is the one Paul describes in 1 Corinthians 3 when he acknowledges that different kinds of communication are needed for different stages of maturity.

If our children are young, we shouldn't expect them to grasp the insights from our favorite Oswald Chambers or Charles Spurgeon devotional book. If our children are older, we don't expect them to stay riveted to a family devotion book full of "little kid" examples.

It's easy to fall into routines with family devotion times, and to some extent those routines are helpful in maintaining the habit and staying simple and consistent. But kids grow and change rapidly, and it's important that our family devotions adapt to their changing developmental needs.

We need to look for moments when we can spiritually stretch each child to the next level of understanding and take the time to assess each child's developing spiritual (and emotional and intellectual) maturity. Are they grasping the key facts of the Bible story? Are they able to move beyond facts to principles that can be applied today? Are they able to make moral and spiritual judgments based on the principles they are learning? Are they developing Christian character as well as mastering information?

The action Bible stories helped me see that it's never too early to start the practice of reading the Bible together as a family. And visits to my grandparents helped me see that this is a practice we need never outgrow. During the last couple of years of my grandparents' lives, I would sometimes take my young family for brief visits. My granddaddy's hearing was failing, and my grandmother could no longer serve up the elaborate home-cooked meals I remembered from my childhood. But we never left their home without my granddaddy asking me if I would read from the little devotional book beside his recliner and then read from the worn Bible that lay under it. I still remember him leaning in close to me so he could hear better, and I read as loudly as I could, knowing I'd have to explain why to my children later. Then we'd hold hands and pray, and as we prepared to leave, my granddaddy would remind me that reading the Bible and praying together as a family is important. And as I looked from his eyes into the eyes of my children, I knew he was right.

7. Combine Information and Application

And remember, it is a message to obey, not just to listen to. If you don't obey, you are only fooling yourself. For if you just listen and don't obey, it is like looking at your face in a mirror but doing nothing to improve your appearance. You see yourself, walk away, and forget what you look like. But if you keep looking steadily into God's perfect law—the law that sets you free—and if you do what it says and don't forget what you heard, then God will bless you for doing it.

James 1:22–25

According to the Bible, spiritual maturity and God's blessing come from both understanding God's Word and applying it to life. The Bible is full of facts, principles, promises, commands, examples, illustrations, warnings, and more—and all that information is designed for life application. Weaving understanding and application together can make a family devotion time dynamic. The big question of every family devotion session should be, Since that is true, then what should I do?

We parents may be too reluctant to challenge our kids to start obeying God's Word as soon as they hear it. We may reason that they're still growing in their faith and that applying the Bible to daily life is a pretty mature skill. But kids are smart, and if we say something is true but don't ask them to act as if it's true, then they categorize it as fable, fiction, or platitude.

Let me illustrate by describing our sons' salvation experiences. One night our family devotional time led us into a discussion of heaven and what it takes to get there. We had discussed salvation many times before but had been careful not to manipulate a decision from our sons, all of whom I thought were probably too young to fully understand their spiritual condition. On this particular night our youngest son, Ethan, was asking the most questions, and to my surprise, our oldest son, Caleb, was chiming in with answers. He rather matter-of-factly told Ethan about sin and hell and trusting in Jesus and going to heaven.

Sensing a teachable moment, I gently asked Caleb, "Do you think that might be a decision you'd want to consider sometime?" He looked at me with some surprise and said, "Oh, Dad, I did that a long time ago." He then described in some detail a night when one of our Bible stories had explained what Jesus did on the cross. He pointed to a specific rocking chair in our family room and said he had crawled behind that chair and asked Jesus to forgive him of his sins and come into his heart. He explained what it meant to be a Christian in such simple but accurate terms that I was left almost speechless.

When Beth and I later did the math and put together the details of his account, we realized that he was five and a half years old when he crawled behind that chair and made that life commitment. He had heard the gospel message, decided it was true, and without even telling his parents, he had applied the truth of the Bible to his own life.

Now fast-forward with me about four years to another family devotion time. This time our youngest son, Ethan, told us that after the previous night's devotion he had recognized that he wasn't a Christian yet and that when he had crawled into his bed that night, he had asked Jesus to forgive him of his sins and come into his heart. The previous night's devotion had been on baptism, and it had led Ethan to ask the rest of the family, "So let me get this straight—am I the only one here who's not going to heaven?"

> **The big question of every family devotion session should be, Since that is true, then what should I do?**

Now that Ethan had made his commitment to Christ, he was eager to be baptized—something that neither of his two older brothers had yet done, though they had both committed their lives to Christ. You see, though Caleb had demonstrated an unusual spiritual sensitivity at a young age, his basically shy personality had made him uncomfortable with the idea of public baptism. Now Ethan's conviction (that when you give your life to Jesus, you get baptized!) became one more piece of information that called for an application.

About a month later, on Thanksgiving weekend, I had the privilege of baptizing all three of my sons on the same Sunday morning. One by one the Bible's gospel message had penetrated their hearts and led them to salvation. And then the command to be baptized had registered with all three at once.

My oldest son was ready for application of the gospel message much earlier than I expected, and he was ready for application of the baptism command much later than I expected. My youngest son was ready to act on both salvation and baptism right away. Because our family devotions had consistently offered information and application, our sons were able to accept the truth and act on it in God's timing for their unique personalities.

I'm eternally grateful that God used our family devotional times to draw all three of our children to Christ. And these times have continued to be among the richest of our lives together, serving as bedrock for times of change and challenge, both positive and negative. A regular devotion time can energize the spiritual life of a family. And when a family finds ways to consistently digest the Bible together, it sets the stage for many other positive spiritual practices.

Please *Do* Try This at Home

1. If you haven't already established a family devotional time, plan a specific date to start one within the next month. Give yourself enough time to visit a Christian bookstore, either in person, online, or through a catalog. Choose one or two resources that are described as appropriate for your children's ages. Let it guide you, along with the suggestions from this chapter.

2. If you do already have a regular devotional time with your family, accept the challenge of making it more and more customized to the needs of your family. Use it to stretch each child to the next level of spiritual growth.

3. Consider writing your own family devotional book based on your family's experiences and spiritual insights. That may sound like a huge undertaking, but it doesn't have to be perfect and it doesn't have to be for anyone's eyes besides your family's. If your kids are old enough, assign them each to write one of the daily devotions, based on a formula you give them from a devotion book you already have. After they've written and delivered that devotion successfully, assign another one. Make sure you do your share as well. Consider making a completed volume of your family devotions a gift to a grandparent or some other close family member.

2

Telling the Stories

The Practice of Eating Together

The way a family learns to do mealtimes at home is usually the by-product of past experiences. We all bring with us certain traditions from our childhoods, like where Dad sits, who says grace, how food is distributed, and whether you serve the food out of serving bowls or cooking pans.

Then we go to school and usually learn to eat cafeteria style, where self-service is the rule. Every tray is an island, and every island joins an archipelago of other self-serving islands at a huge table. School can also teach us all kinds of new mealtime customs, such as whether we avoid belching at the table all the time or only in mixed company.

And if Mom and Dad lived on their own before marriage, they may have picked up other unique eating habits during the single life. For instance, before I was married I developed the habit of having two prepackaged cupcakes and a Coke for breakfast. While my new bride was amazed at my disregard for nutrition, she joked that she could easily serve me breakfast in bed every morning. She'd just keep the cupcakes in the nightstand and the Coke in a cooler, and when I woke up she'd toss them to my side of the bed and go back to sleep.

> As parents, we wanted to know something of what our children had experienced at school that day. But our standard questions were doomed to very brief answers.

Of course, when children come along, mealtime changes dramatically again. On one hand, parents often feel obligated to be more formal and family-like. After all, it's not just the two of you grabbing TV dinners anymore, and you do have all those place settings of dishes you got as wedding gifts. On the other hand, there's something about feeding babies and toddlers that makes mealtime anything but formal. My wife still reminds me of the time our two-year-old vomited all over his end of the table and I looked up briefly but just kept eating.

By the time all of our children were past the baby and toddler age and in school, I started to notice a significant change in our family mealtimes. Generally speaking, mealtimes seemed to become quicker and quieter. Just getting us all to the table at the same time was a challenge. We were all off doing our own work or play, and it seemed we had less and less time to eat between commitments. Once we were at the table, it seemed to be a race to see how quickly we could gobble down dinner and get back to whatever we were doing.

Of course, as parents, we wanted to know something of what our children had experienced at school that day. But our standard questions were doomed to very brief answers.

"How was school today?"

"Fine."

"Did you do anything interesting?"

"No."

"How did your science test go?"

"OK, I guess."

This was even more frustrating for Beth than it was for me, because she was a teacher, and she knew better than most how much more can go on in a typical school day than the kids were saying.

I mentioned this to my friend Glenda at work and was surprised to hear her laugh. Her two boys were older than my three, and she spoke with the experience of someone who had endured many one-word answers at mealtimes. Glenda told me of a tradition they had started in their family called "school stories." Every evening at dinner, before anyone could leave the table, everyone had to tell a school story from their day. It couldn't just be a sentence or two, and it couldn't just be a rundown of their class schedules. They had to describe something that had happened that day in detail and respond to any questions others at the table might have.

"And they actually *do* that?" I asked.

Glenda's eyebrows rose at the idea that her motherly authority would be questioned on this subject. "They do if they don't want to sleep at the kitchen table that night!" she replied.

Knowing that my wife could deliver that same motherly look, I decided we should give it a try.

Ever since that next night, our family has practiced the habit of school stories—intentionally talking about at least part of our day every night at dinner. At first our boys thought it was kind of annoying and stupid. OK, they still think that sometimes. But we have remained devoted to the discipline of everyone talking around the dinner table. The homework waits, the TV and computer stay turned off, and the phone goes untouched until we've been around the table and everyone has told a school story.

Now, as you might expect, the kids quickly turned the tables on us and asked why we didn't have to share work stories or home stories. Now every night at dinner there are at least five stories told around our dinner table.

One night we were just getting ready to sit down for dinner when the phone rang. We gave Caleb permission to answer it quickly and take a message. He did, and after we prayed and started eating, I asked, "Who was that on the phone?"

"Oh, it was just a cosh," he answered matter-of-factly.

"A cosh? What's a cosh?" I asked.

"It's not a what; it's a who," Caleb replied.

"A cosh is a person?" I continued. "What kind of person is a cosh?"

"A pretty nice person, actually," Caleb continued.

"So a cosh is a nice person?" I continued, noticing my wife's knowing smile. I thought I had tripped across some kind of seventh grade jargon that I should have known but didn't. That was OK, except for the fact that my wife seemed to understand, and I couldn't stand being less hip than her.

"So *cosh* is a term meaning a nice person, is that right?" I felt like I was the only person at the table not speaking the language.

"No," my son replied with disbelief. "I don't know what a cosh is—but Aakash is my friend from school—he's from India."

That story about Aakash typifies the kind of discoveries our family routinely makes around the dinner table as we practice this habit of intentional updating and communicating with one another. I meet one of our son's friends whom Beth knows about but I don't. The family hears about a stress at work that I normally would just keep to myself. A teacher who has done something creative or inappropriate gets our attention.

On rare evenings when everyone is in a good mood at the same time, and talkative, school stories can be a highlight of the week. On other evenings it can be like pulling teeth just to get everyone to say something. Either way, the habit of eating together and (just as important) talking together has become one of the main practices that helps keep our home team together. School stories inevitably produce laughter, discovery, empathy, and understanding. They give the family permission to communicate and a format in which to do so. And we've not found a better, more disarming place than around the dinner table.

> The habit of eating together and (just as important) talking together has become one of the main practices that helps keep our home team together.

> How happy are those who fear the LORD—
>> all who follow his ways!
> You will enjoy the fruit of your labor.
>> How happy you will be! How rich your life!
> Your wife will be like a fruitful vine,
>> flourishing within your home.
> And look at all those children!
>> There they sit around your table
>> as vigorous and healthy as young olive trees.
> That is the LORD's reward
>> for those who fear him.
>
> Psalm 128:1–4

I love this picture in Psalm 128 of a happy, healthy family. And I don't think it's an accident that this family snapshot

37

is taken within the home and around the table. Depending on your family's situation, you may find breakfast or bedtime or some other time or place more conducive to family fellowship and communication. But if you can swing it, I'd suggest carving out dinner as the time and place for this important practice and protecting it as family time at least four or five times a week. It's a time of relief from the work of the day. And it's a time when the satisfaction (and distraction!) of food and the security of family can create a climate of openness for communication.

There's a moment almost every evening just before dinner when our family sits down at the table together and extends our hands to one another to pray and thank God for the meal and the blessings of the day. It's a moment when I often remember that the richness of my life is around that table and that this is "the LORD's reward for those who fear him."

Have you discovered the benefits of a regular meal with your family? Here are some things we've discovered that can make a time like that most meaningful and effective.

Helping Your Family Practice Eating and Talking Together as a Home Team

1. Choose a Meal When Your Family Can Have the Most Time Together

They worshiped together at the Temple each day, met in homes for the Lord's Supper, and shared their meals with great joy and generosity.

Acts 2:46

If we're already struggling to find time each day to read together or have family devotions, we may find it challenging to carve out a second time when our families can talk together about what's going on in our lives. That's why a mealtime can be so well suited to both feeding the family and feeding the family's fellowship. And for most families, the evening meal will provide the most quality time to embrace this practice.

Of course, work and travel schedules can sometimes keep families from being together consistently at dinnertime. In that case, we might need to find another time to work on family communication. We might also choose to reevaluate our work, play, or travel situation and ask ourselves if those priorities are worth the sacrifice of not having dinner together regularly. Reserving at least one meal a day for the family can be one of the best life investments we make, even if it means a little less money or slower career advancement.

However we carve out the time, the important thing is to create a fairly consistent setting in which communication about the day can freely flow without feeling forced. When our children were younger, for example, Beth would always have "circle time" with them when they returned home from school or preschool. Whoever was home at that time would gather around in a circle while the ones who had just come home from school unpacked their backpacks or schoolbags and showed what they had worked on that day.

For most families, the evening meal will provide the most quality time to embrace this practice.

As our guys got older, circle time evolved into "homework time," where they unpacked not only what they did in each subject that day but also what was due the next day in school. This habit has proven to be good not only for their performance in school but also as a lead-in to informal dialogue about things that happened during the day.

It's not surprising that the early church family met both for the Lord's Supper and for shared fellowship meals. In fact, at one point Paul had to scold the Corinthian church for combining the vertical, worship purpose of the Lord's Supper with the horizontal, fellowship purpose of mealtime (see 1 Cor. 11:20–22).

We could, of course, combine the practice of reading or having family devotions together with the practice of talking together and staying current on one another's lives. But mealtimes add so much to the atmosphere of opening up and sharing that I believe it's far better to preserve the family devotion time as a separate commitment and allow the family mealtime to provide the setting for carefree communication.

2. Create a Simple Format for Sharing

But if we are living in the light of God's presence, just as Christ is, then we have fellowship with each other, and the blood of Jesus, his Son, cleanses us from every sin.

1 John 1:7

The Bible says that when we confess our sins to God, it's like emptying the dark parts of our lives out into the light. This reestablishes fellowship not only with God but also with one another. By providing simple formats for "confessing" the day's activities to our families, we build fellowship within our families and help counteract the bad habit family members can have of keeping things bottled up inside.

The school stories idea is one example of a simple format that can facilitate family sharing. Another one we use from time to time is called "high point, low point." Family members are asked to share the high point of their day (the best or most interesting thing that happened) and the low point of their day (the worst or most boring thing that happened).

High point, low point is especially useful when someone isn't in the mood to share a school story. Standard formats have the advantage of being predictable and easy to follow, but they can have the disadvantage of growing stale after a while. So be ready with some alternate ways that your family can share information without having to think too hard about it.

One format we've used for sharing high points is a bright red plate (sold in a number of department stores and gift shops) that has printed around the edge, "You are special today." We use it for birthdays, report cards, anniversaries, big game victories, promotions, accomplishments, and any other reason remotely worth celebrating. When someone comes to dinner and sees the red plate at his place, he not only feels honored but also knows he has a high point to talk about at dinner that night.

Whatever format we use, the objective is not to interrogate or cross-examine but to gently shine a light of warmth and acceptance that encourages each family member to empty his or her emotional pockets and place victories and hurts out on the table for everyone to share.

3. Model Authentic, Vulnerable Communication

I don't mean to say that I have already achieved these things or that I have already reached perfection! But I keep working toward that day when I will finally be all that Christ Jesus saved me for and wants me to be.

Philippians 3:12

Nothing will promote open and honest communication from our children like our own open and honest communication. If dinnertime develops into a one-way interrogation time, it will soon be no fun for anyone. But when parents model the kind of authentic communication they long to see from their children, they take a powerful step toward teaching those children a relational skill that will serve them their whole lives.

I've been amazed at how maturely our kids, at all ages, have responded to concerns or victories that we have shared with them during family talk times. Often something I'll mention in passing during dinner will come up again during family devotions when one of the kids is praying. It means a lot to me to know that they were listening to my life concerns just as I was listening to theirs and that they would carry that concern to God in prayer.

Paul wrote to his "children" in the Philippian church that he wasn't perfect but that he was very much still in the process of becoming what Christ wanted him to be. When we communicate openly and vulnerably like that with our children, we give them permission to be imperfect too, and we invite them to join us in helping each other grow.

In his wonderful book *The Purpose-Driven Life*, author Rick Warren writes about the power of humility and the willingness to admit our weaknesses: "If all people see are your strengths, they get discouraged and think, 'Well, good for her, but I'll never be able to do that.' But when they see God using you in spite of your weaknesses, it encourages them to think, 'Maybe God can use me!' Our strengths create competition, but our weaknesses create community."[1]

> **The more involved parents are in their children's lives, the less they have to learn from school stories or dinner conversations.**

It's that sense of community that is the goal of family talk times. It's a sense of openness that comes only in an environment of security and authenticity. That doesn't mean that Dad dumps every problem from work at the dinner table or that Mom worries the children with how little money is in the checkbook. But authentic community does mean that everyone in the family shares at least some of what's going on in life at more than a superficial level.

4. Pray Your Way into Their Day

Keep on praying.

> 1 Thessalonians 5:17

If we want our families to connect at the dinner table, then the most productive thing we can do is make sure we're connected by prayer between meals. We must know the schedule and demands each family member faces during the day and pray for them during key times each day.

Some parents I know write notes in their children's lunches or, when they're older, call them during the day to let them know they're praying for them. Others have key times in their families' lives written into their calendar or on sticky notes beside their telephone or computer.

Beth has always been an active volunteer in our children's classrooms at school and at church. I know many parents who are booster club volunteers, coaches, den mothers, or activity sponsors at school. The more involved parents are in their children's lives, the less they have to learn from school stories or dinner conversations.

The point is that communication and fellowship between family members doesn't just take place at mealtime. It can take place throughout the day as we are involved in our families' lives and as we pray our way into each other's day. It's there that we empathize with the lives they're living apart from us. Then when we're reunited for school stories or high point, low point, our questions and our insights into what our children are and aren't saying are much more acute.

5. Remain Consistent but Not Legalistic

You are trying to find favor with God by what you do or don't do on certain days or months or seasons or years. I fear for you. I am afraid that all my hard work for you was worth nothing. Dear friends, I plead with you to live as I do in freedom from these things.

Galatians 4:10–12

In his letter to the Galatians, Paul reminds us that laws and traditions governing outward behaviors are really designed to mold obedient hearts into a readiness for spiritual freedom. In the same way, mealtime traditions and habits can help our family members understand and empathize with one another and draw us out of our own little worlds so we can learn to see and treat others with Christ-like concern.

Once we've established a pattern of using a daily meal to catch up with one another, we may find it isn't necessary to go through a reporting routine every evening. Sometimes days aren't exciting, and sometimes the family isn't in a talkative mood. Our family doesn't do school stories every night, especially if someone is exhausted or not feeling well.

The important thing to note each day is whether anyone is sullen or withdrawn and whether you know, in general, what's going on and how each person's day went. Of course, you may also find that once you get into the practice of everyone talking about his or her day, it becomes a natural dinnertime routine that you no longer have to prompt.

Please *Do* Try This at Home

1. Identify a time when your family can spend at least thirty minutes together every day, preferably over a meal and preferably at dinnertime. Commit to developing that time as a balanced, family-focused time when everyone talks in turn and everyone listens respectfully. If it's impossible to find a daily time, then identify at least two to three times during the week

when you could catch up with each other—even if it means a conference call!

2. Choose a date when your family will start a tradition such as school stories; circle time; or high point, low point that guides each family member in a process of sharing something that happened that day and how he or she felt about it. Make the tradition simple, with ground rules that are easy to remember and abide by. No matter how many groans you may hear when you announce the new tradition, stick to it for at least two or three months. Let family members suggest alternative methods or ground rules, but make sure it results in everyone sharing in a meaningful way.

3. Ask yourself how vulnerable you have been with your family about your own daily demands, and plan two or three things to share about your life these days that will show your family you're committed to authenticity and openness. And don't limit what you share to cares and concerns. Be ready to share with your family some of your successes and dreams, and model for them the kind of sharing you hope they'll eventually embrace themselves.

3

Making the List

The Practice of Playing Together

I sat in front of my home computer screen, quickly and quietly pecking away. It was early Saturday morning, Beth was still asleep upstairs, and our three young boys were temporarily occupied with Pop-Tarts and cartoons. Now was my chance to get some work done. Now was my chance to catch up on some of the many, many things for which Monday through Friday never seemed to be enough time.

Just as I was getting into a groove, my three sons burst into the room. I confess cringing a little, because I knew the first question that would come, in unison, from their lips.

"Dad, what can we do?"

Foolishly I tried the answers that had stopped working a long time ago. "Well, you can watch a video, you can play outside, you can draw or paint . . ." I knew I wouldn't get very far into that list—I was just stalling so I wouldn't have to take my eyes off my work yet.

"No, Dad. What can we do with *you*? You know what we mean . . ."

I did know what they meant. Any of those activities I had just listed might be acceptable—if I stopped what I was doing and did it with them. They didn't just want to do something. They wanted to do something with me. It was time for evasive maneuver number two. Wheeling around in my swivel chair, I continued with a serious tone.

> **They didn't just want to do something. They wanted to do something with me.**

"Well, guys, Dad's got some things he needs to work on this morning. Maybe I could do something with you this afternoon."

My eight-year-old's face clouded over. My three-year-old started into something between a whimper and a whine. But my six-year-old, the one who was already showing signs of being highly focused and driven like his dad, was ready to face the battle.

"Dad, I thought Saturdays were for fun. I thought you only had to work during the week when you're at your office. Mom said Saturdays are family days."

OK, now he was swinging some pretty big clubs. And he was reasoning like an adult, so he had to be reasoned with like an adult. I reached into my nearby briefcase and pulled out The List.

My computerized project list at that time was about nine pages long. It went about eighteen months into the future and contained projects and responsibilities related to work, church, home maintenance, and other hobbies and interests. The list manager software I was using enabled me to categorize, organize, prioritize, rank, rerank, and—most important—check off when complete.

For about five minutes I explained how the list worked. I showed them all the categories of things I was trying to balance, how important most of them were, and how many things were behind schedule.

My three-year-old peeled off about thirty seconds into the presentation. My eight-year-old just started staring at the floor. But that six-year-old had his next question ready, and it pierced my heart.

"So what do we have to do to get on that list?"

Now in a perfect world, and if I were a perfect dad, I suppose that scene would have ended with me turning off the computer, giving each of the kids a big hug, and going off to do whatever they wanted to do for the rest of the day. But however unnecessarily pious my list presentation had been, the truth was that I needed at least an hour and a half of uninterrupted time that morning to meet the commitments I had made to other people. I would have loved three to four hours, but I *needed* ninety minutes. It was one of those tension points when we're faced with the need to balance our family responsibilities with our work responsibilities.

"You're right, son, you guys should be on the list—very high on the list. In fact, I think you need your own list!"

My eight-year-old's eyes lifted from the floor. The six-year-old looked interested but suspicious. The three-year-old was long gone, watching another cartoon.

I turned back to the computer, opened up a new list, and started asking my two older guys questions. "What are your favorite things to do with me?" I asked, my fingers poised over the keyboard. They looked at me with blank expressions, looked at each other with "Is he serious?" skepticism, then started firing off a list of do-it-with-Dad fun stuff: Take the commuter train downtown, play tennis, go to the zoo, play baseball in our big side yard, go to the McDonalds that has a huge arcade and playground and get

49

Happy Meals . . . The semiautomatic barrage of boredom beaters came faster than I could type them in.

When they finally slowed down, we had a list of over fifty things they'd like to do with their dad—today if possible. But I was able to convince them that you simply can't get everything done in one day. That's why you have to organize and categorize so you can prioritize and do the most important things first.

So we created categories: inside versus outside activities, things you do at home versus things you have to drive to, things that take less than two hours versus things that take up to half a day or most of a day. Within just a few minutes, the list was categorized and organized.

While two copies were printing out, I reached into my desk and pulled out a set of pens and highlighting markers. My sons were still a little uncertain about exactly what I was doing. But now they were smiling, their eyes were sparkling, they were giggling at thoughts of the fifty possibilities we had just rattled off together—and they knew they had their dad's attention.

"Now, you know we can't do everything on this list today," I continued. "So I want you to go to the kitchen table and use the pink highlighter to color the things you'd really like to do today. Use the yellow highlighter to color things you'd like to do second best and the blue highlighter to color things you wouldn't mind waiting a while to do. Then rank all the pink things in order by writing 1, 2, or 3 beside them. Then rank the yellow things and then the blue. Then bring the list back to me. We'll rank it in the computer and choose at least the top two or three things that we have time for today."

As the boys howled and ran out the door to the kitchen, they almost bowled over their mother, who was standing sleepily at the door.

"What are you guys up to?" she asked with good-natured suspicion.

"We're prioritizing!" they called over their shoulders on the way to the kitchen. When I explained what we had just done, Beth rolled her eyes and shook her head with a smile. Her lists are generally a little shorter than mine—the kind you stick on the refrigerator door with a magnet—and she considers my computerized list a mostly male and marginally compulsive behavior.

I guess my boys proved her right. It took them almost an hour and a half at the kitchen table to agree on their carefully ranked list. When they returned it to me, I was just finishing up what I needed to get done that morning. We updated their list and set out to do the top thing on it.

Of course, ever since that Saturday morning, I've been forced to face that list. But it's worthwhile because I really do want my children to be at the top of my list, right under my God and my wife. Plus, my children now know a little bit more about how to manage their own priorities. It seems to mean a little more to them now when they see me choose to put them at the top of my list. And I'm trying to do that more and more often.

———————

Maybe it's a cliché, but the family that plays together really does tend to stay together. And there's nothing more natural for a home team to do than play. Yet our lives get busy and our responsibilities get heavy, and unless we recognize and value the many benefits of play, we will always put it off until we have spare time. Families deserve and need so much more of what play has to offer than spare time usually allows. Making time for play can literally bring our families increased health and happiness.

It's when we are playing together that we set aside the cares and weights and anxieties of life, even if only for a while. Playing together helps us not take the world so seriously, and it helps us remember that our work, our education, our finances, our home projects—all the things we have to tear ourselves away from in order to play—are not ends in themselves but should really help our families enjoy meaningful lives together.

Play can also offer families lots of opportunities to develop healthier lifestyles. Jogging or playing tennis or golf or even just walking together can be practices that not only give us time for conversation but help us stay physically fit and emotionally bonded together in our love for that sport.

The Bible doesn't have a lot to say specifically about how families should play together. It doesn't tell us how Jesus played with his family, and it doesn't give us a letter from Paul about what games worked best in the early church. One might conclude that there wasn't a lot of time for fun and games during Bible times.

But we do read in the Bible about festivals, dancing, playful music, and laughter. While family life then may have been harder in many ways, we get the definite sense that families have always needed the occasional respite and distraction of play. During one of the most peaceful, prosperous times in Israel's history, King Solomon wrote this in the book of Proverbs: "A cheerful heart is good medicine, but a broken spirit saps a person's strength" (17:22).

> **When a family takes time to play together, it creates a setting in which encouragement and laughter and fun can flow to whoever needs it.**

When a family takes time to play together, they create a setting in which encouragement and laughter and fun can flow to whoever needs it. Playtime can re-energize those whose strength for living has been sapped. Play can help us regain perspective and remind us that laughter can flow in all circumstances, and that our families are an ever available oasis.

Healthy practices like reading together and talking together at mealtimes are like the classrooms in which we can seek to teach Christian principles to our families, but the practice of playing together is more like lab work. It's there that we see how the theory studied in the classroom translates to real life. It's where we see if the truth has its desired consequences.

Have you discovered the benefits of consistent playtimes with your family? Here are some things we've discovered that can make times like that most meaningful and effective.

Helping Your Family Practice Playing Together as a Home Team

1. Be Responsive to Your Children's Requests for Play

Keep on asking, and you will be given what you ask for. Keep on looking, and you will find. Keep on knocking, and the door will be opened. For everyone who asks, receives. Everyone who seeks, finds. And the door is opened to everyone who knocks. You parents—if your children ask for a loaf of bread, do you give them a stone instead? Or if they ask for a fish, do you give them a snake? Of course not! If you sinful people know how to give good gifts to your children, how much more will your heavenly Father give good gifts to those who ask him.

Matthew 7:7–11

In this teaching about prayer, Jesus makes it clear that God is a heavenly Father who loves to respond to his children's requests. And he says it's natural even for less-than-perfect human parents to want to give good things to their children. Play is one of those good things.

I have come to understand that when my children come asking me to play, they are primarily asking for my time and attention. Yes, they enjoy the games themselves, and, yes, they could play most of them without me. Many times they do. That's why it's so important that I respond as often and as positively as I can when they specifically ask me to do something with them. It's not just about the game. It's about the time and the attention.

When I was a child, my dad was a busy pastor of a growing church. And there were plenty of times when his responsibilities kept him from being able to say yes to my requests for play. But when he did say yes, it was special. I remember fondly the times he and I stood out in our front yard and played catch with a baseball. He had a big first baseman's mitt, and at six feet six inches tall, he could reach almost anything I threw near him.

But what I remember most about those times was not really about baseball. I remember doing my very best and listening for his words of approval. I remember throwing as hard and as accurately as I could and trying to catch anything he threw at me. When I threw one at his feet that got past him, I remember running after it and telling him I would get it. I didn't want him to get tired too quickly and cut short our time together.

Not every parent loves games or exercise, and not every schedule allows lots of time for play, but when our children, or spouses, ask us to do something with them, it's worth remembering that they may be asking for more than just play.

2. Budget Time for a Little Play into Each Day

Some children were brought to Jesus so he could lay his hands on them and pray for them. The disciples told them not to bother him. But Jesus said, "Let the children come to me. Don't stop them! For the Kingdom of Heaven belongs to such as these." And he put his hands on their heads and blessed them before he left.

Matthew 19:13–15

In his busy life and ministry, Jesus made it clear that he had time for children. He had time to touch them tenderly and to bless them. It would not surprise me at all if he had time to scuffle with them and play with them. I think that's a large part of how you bless children, or give them happiness. But no matter how busy Jesus was, or how busy his disciples felt he was, he was willing to set aside a little time in his day to focus on children and give them his time and attention.

I almost titled this chapter "From Dinner to Dusk," because that is the time our family has most regularly carved out for play. It's after work, after school, after homework, after helping with dinner and dishes but before bath time, family devotion time, and bedtime. Often that leaves an hour or less, and if I'm traveling or someone has a music lesson or a school event that afternoon, we've found we can't always squeeze playtime in. But I'd say we average three or four days a week, and in that hour or so between dinner and dusk, we've found we can fit in a little driveway basketball, a quick bike ride in the neighborhood, or a few minutes of touch football. When weather keeps us inside, we may resort to Ping-Pong or a quick board game.

Many of the games we play as a family had to be adapted to our situation or our number of players. Some of them we made up altogether. To be practical, a regular family playtime usually has to take place in our home or in our yard, and that often means personalizing the game to the space and time we have. As our children have grown older, we've had to change lots of rules and boundaries. We can't let a fifteen-year-old swing for the fences in baseball like he did when he was a five-year-old.

What has surprised and delighted me over the years is that a few minutes of play each day seem to be enough. Sure, it would always be nice to play longer, but I've found that when we say yes to some play with the qualification that it has a time limit, and especially if it's getting dark outside, that even children are grateful for whatever time allows.

Maybe an early morning jog fits your family situation the best. Maybe a late-night card game or jigsaw puzzle matches your schedule or the ages of your kids. Maybe you're even in the position to play racquetball at noon. The challenge is to not wait for spare time but to schedule time that allows play to be a regular priority in your family schedule.

3. Use Play to Teach Character

Teach your children to choose the right path, and when they are older, they will remain upon it.

Proverbs 22:6

The Bible says that childhood is the best time to learn the right paths of character and conduct. And the times when family members play together provide excellent opportunities to influence maturity and character development. The more children mature in character, the more they should demonstrate things like sportsmanship, teamwork, fairness, honesty, and self-discipline. They should also be learning to give their best, to develop strategies for succeeding, and to persevere even when they're not winning.

> **During that thirty minutes in the backyard, we have more opportunity than we realize.**

Teaching our families how to play involves so much more than game rules and scorekeeping. The field of play is where they develop life skills for the field of competition, the field of academics, the field of work, perhaps even the field of battle. The fairness and compassion and teamwork they learn at home will serve them the rest of their lives, and during that thirty minutes in the backyard, we have more opportunity than we realize.

All of our children can be competitive, but our middle son, Noah, used to have a real challenge with his temper when he wasn't winning. It seemed that no matter what we did to try to teach him that his outbursts were inappropriate, he couldn't get his emotions under control when the game wasn't going his way.

We also observed that even as a young child Noah seemed unusually enamored with money. He was the kind of kid who would stick his fingers in every pay phone or vending machine he saw, with the hope that he would find a leftover nickel or quarter. Once we turned to see him lying flat on his stomach and stretching as far as he could reach under a vending machine in the hopes of pulling out some spare change. The sticky quarter he found seemed to him an ample reward for the filth that covered him when he stood up.

As Noah's temper tantrums on the playing field persisted, we developed the idea of fining him for each inappropriate outburst. Before the game, before his emotions and adrenalin were all pumped up, we told him that any demonstration of temper or poor sportsmanship (by him or anyone else) would result in a fine of fifty cents. Throughout the game we would tally his fines, and when we went in the house he would be asked to go immediately to his room and bring down his fine, to be placed in the penalty cup.

A few months later we all went to Disneyland on the proceeds accumulated in that penalty cup. No, not really. In fact, it only took a few days of consistent fining for Noah's passion for sticky quarters to bring his temper into check. To this day, when I see him compose himself during competition, I'm grateful that we took the time to work on that character trait during backyard baseball.

There are so many life-shaping principles in God's Word that can become part of your family's unwritten rule book. Many of them can be found in the very practical wisdom book of Proverbs. For example, I found these just by skimming one page of Proverbs:

> "A false witness will not go unpunished, and a liar will be destroyed" (19:9).

> "People with good sense restrain their anger; they earn esteem by overlooking wrongs" (19:11).

> "Short-tempered people must pay their own penalty. If you rescue them once, you will have to do it again" (19:19).

> "Get all the advice and instruction you can, and be wise the rest of your life" (19:20).

> "Children who mistreat their father or chase away their mother are a public disgrace and an embarrassment" (19:26).

> "If you stop listening to instruction, my child, you have turned your back on knowledge" (19:27).

> "Avoiding a fight is a mark of honor; only fools insist on quarreling" (20:3).

> "The godly walk with integrity; blessed are their children after them" (20:7).

> "The LORD despises double standards of every kind" (20:10).

> "Even children are known by the way they act, whether their conduct is pure and right" (20:11).

> "Don't say, 'I will get even for this wrong.' Wait for the LORD to handle the matter" (20:22).

That's quite a bit of character-building wisdom just from one page of the Bible! Just think what it would be like to write up a family rule book for playing together that included ten or twenty verses like these. Psalm 119:11 reminds us that hiding God's Word in our hearts helps us avoid sinning against him, and 1 Corinthians

13:11 reminds us that childish ways should give over to mature ways as we grow in Christ. What a difference it could make in the character of our families if our playtimes were consistently regulated by the principles from God's Word. Our family members' future teachers, coaches, co-workers, and employers will all be grateful for the time we invest in our backyards, using play to teach character.

4. Make It Fun for Everyone (Level the Playing Field)

And now a word to you fathers. Don't make your children angry by the way you treat them. Rather, bring them up with the discipline and instruction approved by the Lord.

Ephesians 6:4

One of the challenges of playing together as a family is the challenge of compensating for different levels of ability. Parents know how to ease up on their advantages of size, weight, or skill when they're playing with their children (usually), but it's more difficult for a thirteen-year-old to hold back on his advantages over a nine-year-old.

If you've ever been in a game where your competitor is far superior, you know that frustration can often lead to anger. In Ephesians Paul writes of the parents', and especially the father's, responsibility to treat children in a way that doesn't inherently make them angry. That helps me remember that during family playtimes it's my responsibility to level the playing field and try to give everyone a fun and challenging experience.

That doesn't mean that someone can't win and someone can't lose. It also doesn't mean that the skill level has to drop to the ability of the smallest or youngest family member. But with a little creativity and effort, parents can craft games and rules that let everyone participate, contribute, and even compete.

For example, when my sons and I play driveway basketball these days, my nine-year-old and I are usually on one team, and my fifteen-year-old and thirteen-year-old are on another team. The older guys can steal my passes or block my shots, but they can't steal their younger brother's passes or shots. (If Mom plays, of course, we all give her the ball as often as possible and cheer whatever she does.)

When the four of us play touch football, I quarterback both sides while the fifteen-year-old and thirteen-year-old guard each other as receivers. The nine-year-old is a defensive lineman who rushes me as the quarterback on every down. That nine-year-old would rather sack me than defend a brother who's a foot taller than him, and I'd rather stand back there and throw than run down the field every time. Everyone has a role in which they can contribute and succeed.

Whether it's a board game or card game, a physical competition or an intellectual challenge, we always seek to choose even sides. Even better are games where we can all be on the same side against some challenge. For example, when we play Ping-Pong or tennis, we can play the traditional singles or doubles, where one side wins and one side loses. But it's often the most fun when we choose to see how many volleys we can make in a row without missing. That puts us all on the same side, without a winner or loser. And that leads in to the final tip for playing together.

5. Focus on Camaraderie, Not Competition

> How wonderful it is, how pleasant,
>   when brothers live together in harmony!
>
> Psalm 133:1

I believe family play is healthiest when competition is not the focus. The Bible says that harmony, not rivalry, makes life pleasant. And everyone knows that a home team is happiest and most effective when there is internal harmony and unity.

> **Families should focus more on the warmth of camaraderie than the heat of competition.**

Certainly learning how to compete with integrity and character is one important benefit of a family playing together. But there is enough sibling rivalry and enough temptation to envy and jealousy in families without allowing family game times to stir it up. The wise writer of the book of Ecclesiastes observed that most people are motivated to success by envy of their neighbors (see Eccles. 4:4), but that kind of success is ultimately meaningless. Families should focus more on the warmth of camaraderie than the heat of competition.

There are many, many places today where families can engage in play for the purpose of competition. But on our home fields, our families should be more like teams that scrimmage internally during the week so that they are unified, disciplined, and ready to compete on game day. That's when our home teams break from the huddle and the members assume their various positions in life. And that's when they wear their character and conduct like a uniform that reflects on our homes, and on our Lord.

If you've ever fallen or been knocked down or injured during a game, you know that one of the most encouraging moments in sports is when your teammates come to your side and help you back to your feet. In that simple gesture they are saying that they care about you, that they're on your side, and that you're in this game together. That's what family play is about. And it's that camaraderie that allows you to keep getting up.

Please *Do* Try This at Home

1. Take a minute to write down a handful of games or sports your family enjoys playing when you have the time. If possible, look for games that can involve the entire family and that require an hour or less. They don't have to be scorekeeping games. Your options could be as simple as playing catch, hitting fly balls, or roller-skating in the driveway. They could be indoor games or outdoor games. Then plan at least one time this week when you and your family can play together. After doing this two or three times, consider how often your family could work play into its weekly schedule.

2. Whether you show it to your children yet or not, take a stab at creating your family's own character-building rule book for family play. You could use the examples from Proverbs listed in this chapter, or you could use your own favorite verses that demonstrate Christian character (Gal. 5:22–23, for example). As you observe areas where your family (or you!) needs to mature in character, look for Bible verses that speak to that need. Incorporate your rule book verses in your family devotions, and use your family play-time as illustrations of those biblical principles.

3. Think individually about each member of your family and his or her particular needs for growth and development. What kind of games or family playtimes could lead him or her toward maturity in those areas? Map out a plan for urging your family toward both maturity and camaraderie as they play together.

4

Finding the Fun

The Practice of Working Together

One morning in late August, our family awoke to something fairly unusual at our house—a completely free Saturday. No ball games were scheduled. No business travel called me away. No church activities beckoned. No homework was incomplete. And much to my sons' delight, no shopping needs required that we go to the mall. We had been so busy leading up to this day that it hadn't even occurred to us to schedule a family outing of some kind. Nothing awaited us but a sunny late-summer day.

"So what are we going to do today?" Noah asked. You might remember from chapter 3 that our middle son, Noah, is the big doer in our family and usually the first one to pose that question if there's any kind of lull.

I'm sure he thought it was a pretty safe question. The lawn was in pretty good shape, and the house was tidy.

Surely what we would do would be something fun. That's why my answer disappointed him.

"I was thinking this is the perfect day to take care of that tree out front," I offered, then braced myself for the reaction.

The tree out front to which I was referring was really just a stump, but it was a seven-foot-tall stump. A few days earlier a violent windstorm had ripped through our area and snapped the tree in half. Large sections of other trees had joined it and filled our front yard with branches and leaves.

"Oh no, not work!" was Noah's predictable reply, and his brothers quickly joined in the chorus.

"This is Saturday!" our oldest son, Caleb, complained. "Besides, I already worked in the hole two days ago."

The "hole" was the brush pile at the bottom of the hill in our backyard where we had dragged and thrown the chopped up branches from the trees a few days before. That quick little family project had taken two to three hours each of the nights we had worked on it, and Caleb's job had been to be the "branch manager" down at the bottom of the hill, where the mosquitoes were particularly annoying.

I assured Caleb that chopping up a tree and digging out the stump would not require that he repeat the hard time he had done in the hole.

"Can we even *do* this? Don't we need to *call* someone?" our youngest son, Ethan, added.

But I was ready with my credentials. "Oh sure, we can do this. Several years ago your mother and I went on a mission trip where we helped some folks clear out trees and pull stumps. I'll show you how to do it. And it will be a lot easier with all of us working on it."

I then told them that for a few minutes they could do whatever they wanted before we were ready to get started. But I expected them dressed for work and out in the front yard in thirty minutes.

The half-hour reprieve gave them time to adjust their Saturday expectations a little, and I was proud of the willing attitudes that reported for work a half hour later. We began by digging out the pile of mulch at the base of the tree, and as we turned the first few shovelfuls over into the wheelbarrow, we discovered some huge earthworms.

"Wow, those are bigger than the ones we get up at the lake!" Ethan exclaimed. "We should take those with us next weekend when we go fishing." His remark reminded me that we were indeed planning to go fishing the following weekend.

So even though it wasn't part of the job, I indulged Ethan's idea and asked him to see if his mom could find us something to store some bait in. A few minutes later he and Beth emerged with a plastic container, and by then we had already found a dozen more worms. Somehow we had stopped digging mulch and started digging worms. In fact, we had to dump the mulch we had already shoveled to make sure we hadn't missed any large worms.

Still, the mulch was getting shoveled, and a few minutes later we had a wheelbarrow full of mulch and dirt and a cottage cheese container full of worms. That's when the work started seeming more like work again. Digging around roots and chopping away with a semisharp ax at the stump's former lifelines was hard, hot work, and the worm harvest no longer provided a fun incentive.

Beth had joined the project too, and we paced ourselves by taking turns shoveling versus raking and hauling dirt. I reminded the boys how much easier this was to do as a team than if any of us were doing it ourselves. But I was getting hot, tired, and bored too. I decided it was time to stop chopping at roots and proceed to fell the tree.

The idea of chopping the tree down restored some of our work crew's enthusiasm. Noah started running up to the trunk and jump-kicking it. Caleb ran inside to get the video camera, and Ethan took some mighty initial whacks with our semisharp ax. I couldn't help but wonder if I left the three of them alone for a while if they wouldn't find a way to either get that tree down or give us a chance at winning some money from *America's Funniest Home Videos*.

The tree trunk was over a foot in diameter, though, and I decided it would take several thousand ax whacks from Ethan or several million kicks from Noah to do what a chain saw could do in a few minutes. Since Caleb was now determined to get Noah on video kicking the tree over, we agreed that I would use the chain saw to prepare the tree for Noah's big kick finale.

For the next several minutes, I sawed and he delivered six or eight ferocious jump-kicks. Then I sawed some more, and he delivered more kicks. Finally, with the tree almost sawed all the way through, Noah was able to deliver the final blow that cracked off the seven-foot stump and sent it crashing to the ground. Of course, then Ethan insisted that we pick up the huge log and balance it on the remaining stump so he could kick it over on camera too. Believe it or not, we did just that.

After more digging and hauling and chopping and raking, the job was eventually finished. We were ready to cool off under the garden hose and go in for lunch. As I had hoped, the consensus around the lunch table was that the Saturday morning work project hadn't been that bad. In fact, we were kind of proud of our accomplishment together. We laughed about worms and fishing and kicking down trees and speculated about how the pictures and video we had shot would turn out. We had enjoyed being together. We had enjoyed working together.

There are a number of ways in which the practice of working together as a family is similar to playing together as a family. Both provide together time. Both can teach teamwork and cooperation and character. And when our children are young, we can sometimes even pass off work as play. To a three-year-old, raking leaves can be just as much fun as playing ball.

But there really is a significant difference between a family game and a family project. Play is something we consume. Work is something we contribute. Play is fun. Work is hard. Play pulls us together for common enjoyment. Work pushes us in the same direction for a common good. Play brings us pleasure. Work brings us satisfaction. Play is like friendship and fellowship in our churches. Work is like ministry and missions through our churches.

> **Play pulls us together for common enjoyment. Work pushes us in the same direction for a common good.**

And, of course, because of these dynamics, play is often embraced, while work is often avoided. It's true in all kinds of families, including church families like the one in Thessalonica:

> Yet we hear that some of you are living idle lives, refusing to work and wasting time meddling in other people's business. In the name of the Lord Jesus Christ, we appeal to such people—no, we command them: Settle down and get to work. Earn your own living. And I say to the rest of you, dear brothers and sisters, never get tired of doing good.
>
> 2 Thessalonians 3:11–12

Like a wise parent, Paul identifies for his "brothers and sisters" not only the value of working and doing good but also the dangers of idleness, laziness, and meddlesomeness. He starts with an appeal, and then it's as if he remembers that when work is involved he needs to make it a command. It's not optional, though for some it is not yet voluntary.

That's certainly what I've found to be true with my family. There are times when some family members recognize the need for work, and perhaps even the value of work. There are many other times when at least some family members need the help and motivation of a clear command to get to work.

I've been encouraged to see that often, over time, less mature workers who must be commanded can gradually transform into more mature workers who volunteer. And it's that maturing process that we want to bring about in our families through the practice of working together.

Each summer our family spends several days in southern Illinois at the country home of Beth's mother. Grandma lives on about ten acres with some woods, a separate barn and garage, a shed, and a lot of yard to mow. Since Beth's dad passed away, her mom does a great job keeping up with the house and all that acreage. And she has occasional help from grown kids and growing grandkids.

The first couple of summers after Grandma became a widow, however, the projects that needed doing around her home were huge. The first summer's work was building an addition onto the house, which Beth's brother J.R. did almost single-handedly, with "go-fer" help from the rest of the family. The second summer the house needed scraping and painting, the kitchen floor needed replacing, and a bathroom needed remodeling.

Our plans were for our family to be there for two weeks, but the first week I needed to be a couple of hours away on a mission trip with our church youth group. When I arrived at Grandma's house, I initially thought Beth had purchased or rented new children along with the power sander and paint supplies. Our kids were scraping and painting and cleaning and organizing—all in summer heat and humidity that produced a heat index of over a hundred degrees.

As I joined in alongside them under J.R.'s patient supervision and tutelage, my surprise and delight only grew. Many of us were doing jobs we had never done before with skills we didn't know we had. We were not only working but also talking and laughing and making memories. From oldest to youngest, everyone found something productive to do, and by the end of that week we were amazed at what we accomplished.

> **We were not only working but also talking and laughing and making memories.**

One of our boys accidentally splattered white paint across his black shorts, and we quickly assured him that we would buy him some new ones. He had rarely—OK, maybe never—needed painting clothes before. The only thing that surprised me more than his not caring about his ruined shorts was that even after we returned home he wanted to continue wearing those paint-splattered shorts. Somehow they had become a trophy of a week at Grandma's when our family had a hot, demanding, hard, wonderful time working together.

Have you discovered the benefits of working together as a family? Here are some things we've discovered that can make a time like that most meaningful and effective.

Helping Your Family Practice Working Together as a Home Team

1. Identify Family Projects That Require Teamwork

Two people can accomplish more than twice as much as one; they get a better return for their labor. If one person falls, the other can reach out and help. But people who are alone when they fall are in real trouble.

Ecclesiastes 4:9–10

69

It's always good for each member of a family to have individual chores or responsibilities that are uniquely his or hers. At our house, for example, Beth has developed a check-mark system by which each of our kids tracks the completion of his various household responsibilities. Each son's recorded work is the basis for his weekly allowance, and each is responsible for completing and recording his own chores.

That kind of responsibility is valuable, but what I'm advocating here are projects that require your family to work together as a team. Not every project is best served by a team approach, but almost every team is best served by a challenging project. So one of the keys is identifying something worth doing that your home team can do together.

Yard work is a great job for families to do together. Painting is another. Cleaning out the garage is my personal favorite. And the older your children get, the more repair work or building projects become options. The important things are that the projects allow everyone to have a meaningful, challenging assignment and that the work requires some degree of togetherness and cooperation.

We have friends whose family tradition is that Saturday mornings are for family work. Another family we know joins with two other families to work together on family projects three Saturday mornings each month. Then they take the fourth Saturday off, or sometimes they work on a service project through their church. Each family gets its projects worked on only one morning a month, but they have quite a crew for that morning, and if the projects are well planned, those families can accomplish things together that they couldn't do separately.

We haven't been able to consistently pull off that kind of Saturday schedule, but we do practice occasional family workdays, or at least work mornings. And we've found that passage in Ecclesiastes to be true. Two people really can accomplish more than twice as much as one. And three are even better, just as a cord of three strands is extremely strong (Eccles. 4:12).

Ecclesiastes says that working together not only provides synergy and efficiency but also encouragement. Working alone can be discouraging and even dangerous. When families work together they can accomplish more, if only because they encourage and help one another to keep going.

When Nehemiah was rebuilding the wall around Jerusalem, he made the masterful management decision of grouping work units by family and having them work on sections of the wall near their homes (see Neh. 4:13–15). Sure, that gave them ownership in the overall project, but I think he also knew that working in families would provide familiarity and encouragement and mutual protection that wouldn't exist otherwise. It was a project uniquely suited for families.

Today families can still benefit from working together on projects that are carefully chosen to pull them together. But as in Nehemiah's day, only part of the benefit is in the project itself. A team can build a wall, but a wall can also build a team.

2. Find the Fun in What Needs to Be Done

Even so, I have noticed one thing, at least, that is good. It is good for people to eat well, drink a good glass of wine, and enjoy their work—whatever they do under the sun—for however long God lets them live. And it is a good thing to receive wealth from God and the good health to enjoy it. To enjoy your work and accept your lot in life—that is indeed a gift from God. People who do this rarely look with sorrow on the past, for God has given them reasons for joy.

Ecclesiastes 5:18–20

A lot of the book of Ecclesiastes seems pretty depressing, but buried right in the middle are these encouraging verses. The writer says that work can and should be satisfying and that happiness in work is a gift from God. When you enjoy your work, time flies because you're having fun.

If you want your family's work together to be enjoyable instead of drudgery, this is the best advice I could give you: Find the fun in what needs to be done. Start with what needs to be done, because if you start with what's fun, you're really planning purposeful play rather than fulfilling work. But after you identify the meaningful work that needs to be done, ask yourself, How could this be made fun?

> **After you identify the meaningful work that needs to be done, ask yourself, How could this be made fun?**

For example, when we clean out our garage, I usually ask our boys to organize the sporting equipment. Handling that sporting equipment and organizing it for easier access is fun for our guys. They'd much rather do that than sweep the floor or straighten the rakes and shovels. So I give them the fun in what needs to be done.

In the story that opened this chapter, you saw how cutting down a tree became fun as we dug for worms and videotaped the big kung fu finale. That's finding the fun in what needs to be done. When the car needs to be washed, we often put on our swimming suits and turn it into a water fight. When the lawn needs to be mowed, we sometimes allow creative "lawn sculpting" that allows the mower to create anything from a smiley face to a volleyball court or baseball diamond. That's finding the fun in what needs to be done.

If you're one of the fortunate, blessed people who has been able to choose your life's work, you've probably chosen something you enjoy doing. Overall, your work is joyful and passes quickly because you've found a way to find a blend of what's fun (at least to you) and what needs to be done. That's the zone you're trying to help your family find when they work together—the zone where work feels very similar to play.

3. Teach a Christ-Centered Work Ethic

Work hard and cheerfully at whatever you do, as though you were working for the Lord rather than for people. Remember that the Lord will give you an inheritance as your reward, and the Master you are serving is Christ.

Colossians 3:23–24

Almost every manager and executive I've ever talked to has agreed with me that if a solid work ethic hasn't been learned at home, it's rarely learned on the job. This attitude and practice of working for the Lord even if no one else is watching is one of the greatest gifts we can give our children.

If we're helping our families find a lot of fun in what needs to be done, work ethic is generally not a problem. But it's critical that we hold our families accountable for working hard even when work is not fun.

Notice the two adjectives Paul uses to describe Christ-honoring work. He says that work should be both hard and cheerful. Ask yourself, Which of those is more difficult to get out of my family? Which is more difficult for me to muster myself?

As we lead our families in the practice of working together, we're likely to find that working hard and working cheerfully are in tension with one another. Accomplishing one or the other is easier than accomplishing both at the same time. When work is too hard, it's not easy to muster cheerfulness. When work is too cheerful, it's not easy to work hard.

A few years ago I went through the most difficult and frustrating experience of my career. A huge project I was managing, one that affected the entire organization, was not going well. There were equipment problems, cost overruns, performance deficiencies, and customer service nightmares. For months and months the hours were incredibly long, yet the failures seemed to outnumber the successes two to one.

Finally we persevered and climbed out of the huge hole we had dug for ourselves. I still felt pretty soiled and unsuccessful as I sat across the restaurant table from our executive vice president, my boss's boss. It was a rare lunch meeting with him, and I was trying not to think about the possibility that my employment might be ending now that I had helped us out of the mess I had led us into.

To my surprise, this seasoned executive started asking me about my family and my upbringing. He asked especially about my father and what kinds of things I felt I had learned from him. My surprise turned to astonishment as he not only complimented me on the past months' work but went on to offer me unexpected rewards and increased responsibility.

Then the reason for this interview became a little clearer. "Over the years," he said, "I've noticed that some guys run out of steam and quit when the going gets tough. Others stay on task longer but turn bitter or disillusioned in the process. More rare are the workers who work hard and stay upbeat until the job is done, no matter how difficult or unsatisfying. They stay teachable and seem to learn from their adversity rather than being conquered by it. I'd love to learn how to coach that into people—that's why I've been asking you all these questions. But you've shown me again that the ones who bring that kind of work ethic to the job almost always bring it from home."

I don't know if I've ever felt more highly complimented in my work than during that surprise lunch. And I don't know if I've ever been more thankful for a home team that taught me a Christ-centered work ethic.

4. Help Everyone Develop Skills and Discover Abilities

God has given each of us the ability to do certain things well.

Romans 12:6

In some ways, the homes my wife and I came from were quite similar. But in at least one very significant way they were quite different. She came from a do-it-yourself type home, and I came from a pay-someone-to-do-it type home.

When I first went home with Beth to meet her family, I was astonished to find that her dad had a whole barn full of tools. In our home every tool we owned was in a kitchen drawer. If it could be built or fixed with a hammer or screwdriver, we might take a shot at it. Otherwise, we'd call a more skilled laborer, which was just about anyone in the world who didn't live in our house.

So I was really puzzled to meet a family like my wife's. To me a tool barn sounded as absurd as a silverware barn or a pot-holder barn. Why on earth would you need a whole barn for tools?

But as we grew in our married life together, I became very grateful that what Paul said in Romans 12:6 about the church family was also true for my family—God has given each of us the ability to do certain things well. For a long time, any fix-it job that took mechanical ability, dexterity, or even intuition got either

> **As families work together, there are many great opportunities to develop skills you don't have and discover abilities you didn't realize you had until you tried.**

hired out or handed over—to my wife. But over the years of doing projects together, first as a couple and then as a family, I've been surprised at some of the things I've learned to do, primarily because my wife persuaded me that we could do it together.

As families work together, there are many great opportunities to develop skills you don't have and discover abilities you didn't realize you had until you tried. Some time ago Home Depot came out with a slogan that I think every family should adopt as they work together: "You can do it. We can help."

When Paul wrote to young Timothy in 2 Timothy 1:5–7, he acknowledged that Timothy had the same sincere faith he had observed in Timothy's grandmother and mother. Building on the foundation of what Timothy had learned from his family, Paul then urged him, "Fan into flame the gift of God, which is in you through the laying on of my hands" (2 Tim. 1:6 NIV). It was as if he was saying, "You've learned some things from your family, and I've taught you some things, and the Holy Spirit has gifted you in some areas that you're just beginning to discover. Now go for it! Don't be timid or afraid. You've hardly tasted all you're capable of with God's help."

While Paul was primarily talking about spiritual gifts and ministry, that same gift discovery and development process can take place naturally as a family works together. We can facilitate our families' discovery of aptitudes and gifts and talents that may be as simple as painting skill or as significant as leadership ability. With God's help, we can fan them into flame as we work together.

5. Celebrate Jobs Well Done

Many sacrifices were offered on that joyous day, for God had given the people cause for great joy. The women and children also participated in the celebration, and the joy of the people of Jerusalem could be heard far away.

Nehemiah 12:43

When the families of Jerusalem in Nehemiah's day finished the huge job of rebuilding the wall, they had quite a party. In fact, if you read the book of Nehemiah, the entire third chapter is a sort of honor roll of which families did what in this amazing project. Nehemiah obviously understood the importance of punctuating hard work and success with an exclamation point of celebration.

As families work together and accomplish things together, it's a great idea to commemorate jobs well done. Celebrations acknowledge the value and worth of the work that is completed and the teamwork that made the project successful. Whether you go out to dinner, have a little ceremony to christen your project, or simply turn the hose on everyone to cool off, it's vital that your family sees your work together as an accomplishment and not just an ongoing process.

In addition to parties or other celebration events, one way to commemorate a job well done is through rewards or compensation. "Payday" at our house is Saturday night after the kids have gone to bed. That's when Beth tallies up the check marks on the refrigerator that represent individual chores and adds any group work projects that we've agreed deserve special rewards.

Then she does something that's become quite special to our family. She lays out each kid's compensation on the kitchen table on top of their individual church offering envelopes. When they come downstairs on Sunday morning, they see rewards for their efforts throughout the week. And they have an immediate opportunity to give back the firstfruits of their labor to God, whom we trust they are increasingly learning to recognize as their true Master.

The Bible makes it clear that one day our heavenly Father will reward us for the work we did as part of his family and that there will be a huge celebration to acknowledge the completion of his work in history (see, for example, Matt. 16:27; 1 Cor. 3:9–14). The way we model work, cooperation, rewards, and the investment of those rewards should say a lot to our families about the true meaning of work.

Please *Do* Try This at Home

1. Analyze the work your family does together, and ask yourself if it draws you closer together in teamwork and cooperation. If not, plan a project within the next month that will draw your family together and challenge them to work both hard and cheerfully. You may want to consider joining another family or two in a project or, better yet, perhaps even offering to help a family or elderly couple who can't do their own yard work or housework.

2. The next time your family works together, tell everyone that you're going to evaluate them on both how hard and how cheerfully they work. Give special rewards to those who excel in either area, or give the whole family a special treat for doing well as a team in those biblical criteria for God-pleasing work.

3. At the end of an upcoming family project, plan a special celebration. It could be as simple as a special dinner, or it could include prizes, a family video recapping the work on the project, special guests, or a family reward such as a weekend trip or tickets to a special event. Also, make sure that your celebration and rewards include some way to honor God with your work by thanking him for the health and safety it took to complete the job and by somehow dedicating the work to him with the firstfruits of your labor.

5

Following the Leader

The Practice of Worshiping Together

Thankfully, there are at least seasons in a family's life when everyone seems to love going to church. The kids love their classes and teachers, Mom and Dad love the music and the preaching, and everyone finds it easy to fit in and serve and give themselves wholeheartedly to the church's mission.

And then there are other times. Maybe it's during the teen years, or maybe it's after moving to a new community. Maybe it stems from one family member's spiritual rebellion or struggle, or from a traumatic event or damaged relationship. Whatever the reason, it may not always be pleasant and easy for a family to consistently go to church together, much less sincerely worship together. But the practice of worshiping together can be the thread that holds a family together even when other healthy practices have fallen by the wayside.

I remember several years ago a friend of mine and I were attending a Christian conference in a large city away from home. It was a huge and truly inspiring conference with dynamic speakers, powerful music, and moving times of commitment. I, along with many others, left each evening session with a renewed dedication to God and to being available to him for his purposes.

As my friend Harold and I walked back from an evening session to our hotel room a few blocks away, we were buzzing with excitement over all we were learning and experiencing. Up ahead, about a block before the entrance to our nice hotel, were the same two guys I had seen each time we walked back and forth to the conference. One stood aggressively out on the corner. The other—the one with only one leg—sat leaning against the building behind him. Both men held cups with a few coins in them and extended them to anyone who passed near them.

When Harold started digging in his pocket, I rolled my eyes in disbelief. He had already given these guys his pocket change on three separate occasions. I was beginning to wonder who would pay for Harold's dinner that night and suspected it might be me.

But before I could urge him past our two "obstacles," Harold had started talking to the first guy. My disbelief then multiplied and my mouth dropped open when I heard him say, "Sorry, I don't have any more with me. But my friend here has some folding money."

Three sets of eyes turned on me to see how I would respond. I resented the position Harold had put me in, but I dug in my pocket and awkwardly handed the first man a dollar bill. By then Harold was waiting for me in front of the second man, who also received my reluctant donation.

As we walked on to our hotel, I only half jokingly told Harold I didn't appreciate him giving away my money like that. He said he just felt like he needed to give, and he offered to pay me back when we got to our room. But for some reason, I didn't want him to do that. In fact, I'd go as far as to say I became a more generous person that night.

You see, on one hand, I didn't want to give those two men my money. But on the other hand, I admired my friend's sincere generosity and didn't want to keep him from doing what it appeared God was moving him to do. I actually felt good about giving them the money, even though I wouldn't have done it without Harold's influence. I was glad to be with him and to have my will softened and my desires modified by following his lead.

I have learned that the kind of influence Harold had on me that night is similar to the kind of spiritual influence I can have on my family. And it has helped me remain faithful to the habit of leading my family to worship together and participate faithfully in church together, even when one or more members of our family are resistant. Whether or not everyone in my family feels like worshiping or feels good about church on a given Sunday, there's something powerful about just being with the faithful, watching their behavior, hearing their songs, and watching their actions. It keeps my family exposed to faithful living, whether we're all ready to "catch it" that week or not.

> **Whether or not everyone in my family feels like worshiping or feels good about church on a given Sunday, there's something powerful about just being with the faithful, watching their behavior, hearing their songs, and watching their actions.**

As with most healthy habits, there are times when the habit of worshiping together is a discipline that sometimes has to come from obedience that is awaiting a bridge to desire. That night with Harold I gave my money primarily because he asked me to give it and because I admired his generosity even though I hadn't yet internalized it myself. In a similar way, there may be periods when my family worships because I ask them to and show them how. It may be some time before their obedience to me transforms into their own heartfelt desire for worship and fellowship.

Let me illustrate with another brief story.

I have a fairly unusual middle name. It's the kind of name you probably can't guess, though usually when I tell people that, they insist on trying and ask for the first letter as a hint. Then I get to watch their brow furrow when I tell them my middle initial is as unusual as the name it begins. My middle initial is Y.

That usually leads my name-guessing contestants to inane guesses like Johann (which doesn't even begin with a Y), Yosemite, or Ypsilanti. Then in frustration they grope into the absurd, guessing that cruel or unusual parents might actually have punished me with a name like Yippee, Yahoo, Yodel, or even Yuck. The truth is that my middle name was the maiden name of my great-great-great-great-grandmother hundreds of years ago—and has been passed down through the generations to lucky male offspring like me with the hope that we'll eventually be able to spell it.

During most of my childhood and teenage years, I was a little embarrassed about my middle name, cringing each time I had to write it on an application or hear a teacher mispronounce it on the first day of school. That's why I cringed when I received an unexpected phone call from the personnel department during the first week on a new job:

"Hello, Nate? This is Tammy down in human resources. What's your middle initial?"

Her question startled me, and I flashed back to all those embarrassing teenage days of spelling and explaining my unusual middle name. But I swallowed hard and answered her question.

"Y."

"Well, because I'm filling out some tax and insurance forms here, and they require your middle initial. What is it?"

"*Y,*" I repeated.

"Well I don't know *why* they need it. I'm just trying to fill out the form and do what I'm told here. Now, what is your middle initial?"

Suddenly, for the first time, I was having fun with my middle name. Somehow, there had never been confusion between *Y* and *why* before, and I decided to indulge in her misunderstanding one more time.

"*Y!*" I said, hoping that my tone wouldn't betray the grin on my face.

"Look," Tammy said, "when you get ready to tell me, you give me a call!" Click.

A few minutes later, I was down at Tammy's desk, apologizing, explaining, and laughing with her. For the next few minutes, Tammy instructed everyone who walked by to ask me what my middle initial is. One by one, we drew others into the fun.

My middle name is Yarbrough, and now I love telling the story of how I got that name and the fun I had learning to talk about it. Today I also love telling the story of how I got the name Christian and the fun I had learning to talk about it. But just as I had to discover my way to talking about my middle name, I had to discover my own path to personal devotion to God and to personal, heartfelt worship. As much as my personal experience with God might draw me to him in worship, I have to remember that my family has to discover their own paths.

> **As much as my personal experience with God might draw me to him in worship, I have to remember that my family has to discover their own paths.**

There's a sense in which worship and church participation is a family heritage that is bestowed like a middle name, but ultimately it has to be personally embraced and valued.

There may be times when it seems one or more members of my family are embarrassed about their faith or their church, when in fact, they may just be searching for a way to make their faith and their unique identity in Christ personal. As Harold did for me that night outside our hotel, my job is to keep my family close to God and his ways and his people. In the meantime, I can trust God to lead them on their own personal paths of heartfelt devotion to him.

If there is one spiritual practice most Christian families are committed to maintaining, it's probably the weekly habit of going to church together. But as we all know, going to church together is not necessarily the same thing as worshiping together. Until I looked it up again recently, I had forgotten that the fourth commandment is so detailed and family focused. It's a commandment that speaks not only to the individual but also to the household.

> Remember to observe the Sabbath day by keeping it holy. Six days a week are set apart for your daily duties and regular work, but the seventh day is a day of rest dedicated to the LORD your God. On that day no one in your household may do any kind of work. This includes you, your sons and daughters, your male and female servants, your livestock, and any foreigners living among you. For in six days the LORD made the heavens, the earth, the sea, and everything in them; then he rested on the seventh day. That is why the LORD blessed the Sabbath day and set it apart as holy.
>
> Exodus 20:8–11

It seems to be very important to God that each member of the household be directly involved in remembering, observing, setting apart, and dedicating one-seventh of his or her week to this intentional practice of resting and connecting with God. It doesn't sound optional, and it doesn't sound like God will be satisfied with the parents representing the family while the rest of the household rides along and tolerates the Sabbath like a ritual.

Different seasons of family life probably require different approaches to this spiritual practice of remembering the Sabbath and truly keeping it holy. There may be times in family life—like when kids aren't on the scene or when they're small and enjoy the children's activities of church—that this seems relatively easily. At other times—like when teenagers are rebelling or when one or both parents get hurt or disillusioned by their church—this may be the practice in which families find the most difficulty remaining consistent. But God's call for families to worship is unwavering:

> Give to the Lord the glory he deserves!
>   Bring your offering and come to worship him.
> Worship the Lord in all his holy splendor.
>
> 1 Chronicles 16:29

Have you discovered the benefits of regularly worshiping together as a family? Here are some things we've discovered that can make a time like that most meaningful and effective.

Helping Your Family Practice Worshiping Together as a Home Team

1. Do Whatever It Takes to Find the Right Church for Your Family

> Then he said to them, "The Sabbath was made to benefit people, and not people to benefit the Sabbath. And I, the Son of Man, am master even of the Sabbath!"
>
> Mark 2:27–28

I love the way the words of Jesus complement the fourth commandment and allow me to see God's heart for the Sabbath and for worship more clearly. The command to keep the Sabbath holy reminds me that God deserves my worship, no matter how busy my schedule or how distracted my heart. But Jesus's words further clarify for me that worship is for my good as well as God's glory. In fact, God created the Sabbath with my physical and spiritual needs in mind. I need a regular cycle of worship and rest to reset my perspective and recharge my batteries. So does every member of my family.

So much of a family's health and happiness hinges on whether they have found the right church home. That's why I don't think it's overstating it to say that parents need to do whatever it takes to find the right church for their family. When our family moved from Illinois to Georgia several years ago, we visited fourteen different churches before deciding where we would be members. Ironically, the first church we visited was the one where we ended up investing our lives. God simply used the thirteen others as confirmation that we had immediately found the right one for us.

Later, after we had settled in at our new church, Beth and I reflected on why it had taken us so long to discern the right church for us. We realized that she and I are drawn to churches in different ways. For Beth, the worship service itself and the pastor's teaching ministry were top priorities. Those are important to me too, but I tend to look for a church that needs help or where I might find some role in which to be used by God. That's important to Beth too, but it's not her top priority.

We could tell after visiting once that the worship and teaching ministry of our church was strong, but it was larger than any church either of us had belonged to before, and I was unsure of whether they really needed our help. But after returning from the thirteen alternatives and visiting for a few more weeks, we began to discover places of service that fit our family.

That experience continues to remind me that different family members can have different priorities and connections with a church and that finding a church with strong connections for everyone isn't always easy for large families. But the reality is that families find churches like that all the time. It may take effort, but it is well worth it.

I know families who, when moving, have not chosen a house until they've chosen a church. They wanted to make sure they lived close enough to their church to be very involved and connected with it throughout the week. I've also known families who have uprooted their relationships and changed churches rather than have one or more family members drop out or tune out. I don't think that's always the right thing to do, and I wouldn't recommend for a second that families become church hoppers when things don't go just right for them. But if the alternatives are dropping out, becoming malcontent, or just going through the motions of attending, then it's possible that moving on to a new fellowship is a better choice.

The point is that leading your family to genuinely worship together is no small challenge, even at a church you love and where your friendships are deep. If you're attending a church where you have to drag your family week in and week out, or where hurts are reopened each time you walk through the door, or where the ministries of the church aren't very relevant to your family, then you will have a very difficult task. While no church is perfect, the first priority in leading your family to worship together is to make sure you're in a church where there are open pathways to worship rather than multiple obstacles.

2. Make a Weekly Sabbath Pleasantly Nonnegotiable

And let us not neglect our meeting together, as some people do, but encourage and warn each other, especially now that the day of his coming back again is drawing near.

Hebrews 10:25

Because the Sabbath was made for people and not the other way around, it's important to do everything we can to find the best possible match between our families and a local church. Having done that, we must remember to observe the Sabbath day by keeping it holy!

It's really tragic when parents, or children for that matter, use their families as an excuse for noninvolvement in worship. Of course, I also find it tragic when a church cajoles its members into hour after hour of activity each week, leaving little time for families to be families at home.

What do I mean by pleasantly nonnegotiable? Simply that we are not going to debate whether our family worships together once a week.

How often should families participate together in worship with other believers? Some would say that's up to the individual family, but if I understand the Bible correctly, the answer to that question is at least once a week. And for our family, we've decided to make at least that minimum standard pleasantly nonnegotiable.

What do I mean by pleasantly nonnegotiable? Simply that we are not going to debate whether our family worships together once a week. We're not going to reevaluate the fourth commandment at a later date. We're not going to ask if everyone who lives at our house needs to go. We're not going to take the summer off. At least once a week, we're going to practice the discipline of worshiping together as a family.

What's the pleasant part of that nonnegotiable practice? Well, in part, it's the nonnegotiable nature of our commitment that makes it more pleasant. When every family member knows the standard and sees it followed with consistency month in and month out, there's little temptation to argue or debate, and that makes things more pleasant for all of us.

But there's also something pleasant about the flexibility in our commitment. While most of the time we worship in our home church, we frequently worship in other churches when we're on vacation or visiting friends or family. One weekend we attended a family wedding that was over twelve hours from our home. The ceremony and brief reception ended Saturday evening, and I had to be back for a meeting that required we drive all day Sunday. That's only happened a few times in our family life, and the first time it did we came up with a little practice we call "church in the car."

Now you may be thinking that church in the car sounds like a bit of a compromise, maybe like church on the golf course or church on the beach. But if you ask our kids, they would say that church in the car demands more of their participation and focus than church in the church.

When our family does church in the car, we plan an order of worship before we begin. It includes singing, prayer, Bible reading, and creative teaching. Everyone in the car leads or participates in some way. One time we went around and had everyone tell a Bible story with as many details as he or she could include without looking in the Bible. When each person finished, everyone else in the car got to ask questions about any part of that Bible story, whether he or she had included it or not. Then we all looked for applications of that Bible story to our lives.

When we do church in the car, we sing the songs that are most meaningful to us, our prayer times are more intimate, and the Bible teaching is more personally applied. We're driving across the country somewhere and being reminded of the beauty and vastness of God's creation. It's actually quite worshipful. It's also quite natural to wonder what it's like to live in the places we drive through and to realize that the people we see out doing something that Sunday morning are not in church and possibly don't know Jesus as their Savior. We can pray for them as we drive by. It's not exactly missions, but it may be a little more than we remember to do in a regular church service.

> **It's very difficult for me to lead my family to worship together if I'm not connecting with God very well myself.**

Church in the car can be meaningful as an occasional change of pace, but the writer of Hebrews reminds us that we shouldn't neglect the practice of meeting together as a body of believers. We need the benefits of encouragement and warning from brothers and sisters in Christ. Church in the car is an emergency method for keeping the commitment to worship together as a family no matter the circumstances. Requiring family worship in a pleasantly nonnegotiable way means you do everything possible not to build resentment or resistance from your family as you seek to do everything possible to truly remember the Sabbath and set it apart as holy.

3. Model Authentic, Sincere Worship

But the time is coming and is already here when true worshipers will worship the Father in spirit and in truth. The Father is looking for anyone who will worship him that way. For God is Spirit, so those who worship him must worship in spirit and in truth.

John 4:23–24

It's very difficult for me to lead my family to worship together if I'm not connecting with God very well myself.

If there is unresolved conflict in our family relationships, if the ride to church was less than civil, or if my words and actions at home are inconsistent with what I say and do at church, then I may be limiting the worship experience my family can have together, even if we're at the right church and attend every Sunday.

Jesus said that God is looking for true worshipers. He said that I truly worship when my spirit—the deepest part of who I am—acknowledges with transparency and awe the worth and value of who he is as revealed in the truth of his Word.

Whether they realize it or not, our families are looking for us as parents to be true worshipers too. They're watching us to see how far we will go toward being sincere and vulnerable and authentic in our own worship. They're looking to us to model how to worship. And they may be looking for permission to take risks in their own worship expression.

Imagine that this past Sunday there was a video camera pointed at you during the entire worship service at your church. Now your family is going to sit down and view that tape and make observations about you as a true worshiper. What would they observe? Hopefully it wouldn't be, "Look. She doesn't like that song . . . We were supposed to be praying, but it looks like he's dozing . . . Look at the way she's sitting and the expression on her face—I don't think she's thinking about what the pastor is saying . . . Why is he reading something else when the pastor is talking?"

In a way, that's a silly exercise, but in reality, it may not be that far from what the Holy Spirit would love to do in our lives. Our participation in worship can be routine, dutiful, polished, even reverent. And those aren't necessarily bad things. But is our worship in spirit and in truth? Are we showing our families what true worship looks like?

I'm not an overly expressive worshiper, and I wouldn't urge anyone to put on righteous acts for others. But as I've grown in my own worship experience, I have found that the subtle position of my hands, the closing of my eyes, the passion with which I sing, and even the occasional tears—are all indicators of the true worship that is taking place in my heart. I don't do these things for my family; I do them for my God. But if my family sees them and feels permission to worship more vulnerably and sincerely, that seems like a good thing.

4. Help Your Children Worship from Where They Are

One day some parents brought their children to Jesus so he could touch them and bless them, but the disciples told them not to bother him. But when Jesus saw what was happening, he was very displeased with his disciples. He said to them, "Let the children come to me. Don't stop them! For the Kingdom of God belongs to such as these. I assure you, anyone who doesn't have their kind of faith will never get into the Kingdom of God." Then he took the children into his arms and placed his hands on their heads and blessed them.

Mark 10:13–16

Jesus made it clear that children don't need any training or protocol to come into his presence. To the contrary, he said we adults could learn some things about coming to God from the childlike faith we observe in little ones.

It's important for us as parents to avoid communicating that worship is something you can only do correctly after you're grown up. Many churches help facilitate family worship through children's sermons, special programs, special children's worship guides, or even children's church. But even if a church has an adult-centered worship service, we can still help our children know how to engage as participants and not just endure as long-suffering bystanders.

Sometimes it's as simple as explaining to our children what's happening in the worship service and why we're doing it. Sometimes it's encouraging them to sing or showing them how to use a hymnal or follow along in a church bulletin. If they're old enough to comprehend the morning message, we can help them learn how to take notes. If they're not, maybe a Bible storybook or children's Bible would be more helpful to them during the message.

In the previous chapter I described the way my wife and I pay our children on Saturday night so they can prepare their offering envelopes on Sunday morning. At the close of the service when the offering is taken, Beth usually distributes the offering envelopes each of our boys has prepared. Besides singing, the offering is one of the most participative worship practices there is, and if our families are literally giving from their own earned wages, there is no more important act of worship to teach them than the act of giving back to God financially.

Another is the practice of communion, or the Lord's Supper. I remember the first time one of our boys was passed the plate of bread. He leaned over to his mom and whispered, "Is that manna?"

Worship services are opportunities for learning and understanding, but they should primarily be opportunities for participation. With a little help from us parents, children of any age should be able to find ways to connect with God and express their love to him.

Since our boys were very young, and even now that they are teenagers, I have tried to remember to encourage them each week, "Look for at least a moment during the worship service when you can sincerely tell God how great he is and that you love him." All of us should be able to find moments like that. And the more we experience God's love and faithfulness, the more moments like that there should be in our worship.

5. Identify and Expel False Gods from Your Home

Instead of believing what they knew was the truth about God, they deliberately chose to believe lies. So they worshiped the things God made but not the Creator himself, who is to be praised forever.

Romans 1:25

The reality is that we all know how to worship. Our families know how to worship, even the smallest children. We are born with an innate need to worship. Worship is giving worth and value and respect and love to someone or something. None of us has a problem giving worship. We're just tempted to give it to the wrong things.

Because of that sad reality, one of the key responsibilities we have is to identify idols and get them out of our homes. Anything that dethrones God in our lives is an idol. Anything that we place before him is a threat to our spiritual and physical well-being.

Again and again the Bible warns us not to let our hearts turn away from the Lord to worship other gods (Deut. 11:16) and not to worship in the way pagan people do (Deut. 12:4). There is a clear and present danger that comes from giving things value ahead of God. And it's not just the destructiveness of those things but the fact that they threaten to displace our personal relationship with God, which should be our top priority. "You must worship no other gods, but only the LORD, for he is a God who is passionate about his relationship with you" (Exod. 34:14).

On one hand, we don't want to make every baseball card, video game, or favorite outfit into a guilt trip. On the other hand, God has a track record of being pretty severe with idols and rivals.

There may be times in our families' lives when we need to gently but firmly challenge someone to consider whether something is becoming too important, too demanding of their all-consuming attention and passion. There may be other times when we have to exercise tough love and throw some things out. It won't be easy, but it's worth it. The fourth commandment can be obeyed only if the first three are placed before it.

Please *Do* Try This at Home

1. After church next Sunday discuss the worship service with your family. Ask them to reflect on when they felt most connected with God during the service and when they may have felt they were just going through the motions. Discuss what you could do as a family to better prepare for true, spiritual worship and to remove some of the barriers or distractions. Make plans to implement those ideas the following Sunday.

2. Help your family plan a worship service at home, or in the car on a trip, where everyone participates in some way. Tell them they have an opportunity to plan things that are most helpful to them in expressing their love and worship to God. Make sure they know it doesn't have to last an hour when it's just your family; in fact, it will probably be much shorter than that. Afterward, have each member of the family share what he or she liked best about the worship service you planned and what wasn't as effective as a worship service at church. Also, ask your family if there are ways they feel comfortable expressing their worship at home but not at church or vice versa. Discuss what it is that makes us willing to risk different expressions of worship at different times and places.

3. Write down the names of each member of your family, and alongside each name write down the things

you feel they love and value most. Is there anything on the list that risks becoming more important to that person than his or her personal relationship with God? If so, think through how you could lovingly confront that family member and urge him or her to place God first in his or her life.

6

Going the Distance

The Practice of Traveling Together

As our fifth wedding anniversary approached, Beth and I decided we'd return to the romantic lakeside lodge where we had spent our honeymoon. Of course, things would be a little different this time. For one thing, that lodge was over eight hours away, and we now had a two-year-old toddler and a six-week-old baby. It wouldn't exactly be a second honeymoon. It would be more of a first "familymoon."

To complicate things a little more, two-year-old Caleb had just been to the doctor with an ear infection and was just beginning potty training. Six-week-old Noah was not yet sleeping through the night and tended to cry a lot during the day. But both boys traveled well in their car seats, and we reasoned that Caleb's medicine could travel with us and that both boys were portable enough for us to still enjoy the weekend away.

So off we drove, our little family stuffed in a little car for a little road trip. About a half hour down the road, Caleb notified us that he needed to tinkle, and Beth reminded me that he was too young to "just hold it" as I suggested and that part of the success of potty training was responding instantly to the child's need. So although all our previous experience with potty training had been indoors, I quickly pulled off to the side of the road so Beth could jump out and let our son answer nature's call.

It was a very windy day, and as Beth vanished out of sight, it occurred to me that, being a woman, she might not realize all the physical dynamics of a little boy going to the bathroom outside on a windy day. With cars whizzing by on the highway, our own car still running, and our baby starting to cry in the backseat, I wasn't sure Beth could hear me. Still, I shouted out to the bush they had vanished behind, "Point him downwind!"

"What?" Beth replied, and then immediately afterward I heard her exclaim, "Ohhh nooo!"

There was a brief pause, and then she emerged holding our sheepish two-year-old at arm's length and looking down at her shoes, which had just been sprinkled.

"Why didn't you say something earlier?" she complained, and my explanation—that the whizzing was louder on the highway than behind the bushes—didn't seem to amuse her. From that point on, each time we made a pit stop for potty training, we looked at each other and repeated our new family vacation mantra: "Point him downwind!"

After over ten hours of stop-and-go driving, we finally arrived at the lodge and checked in. The rooms seemed smaller than we remembered, but of course, on our honeymoon we didn't have strollers, swings, and portable cribs to occupy all the available floor space.

Though we were exhausted from our daylong trip, we headed out to the restaurant for dinner and discovered that a few other things had changed as well. On our honeymoon we had always managed to secure a quaint table for two by the window overlooking the lake. But when we arrived with our two small children and all the bags and paraphernalia required to transport them and clean up after them, we were quickly and discreetly guided to a table in the back corner between the doors to the kitchen and the stockroom. It was a restaurant location we became very familiar with over the next few years.

One of the things we had loved about the lodge's restaurant was the huge buffet of southern-style foods. So it seemed like a real treat to order two buffet meals—until, of course, we realized that multiple plates and bowls and glasses were only half the challenge we now faced. With two tired, cranky little guys now in tow, one of us had to shuttle food from serving line to table while the other sought to contain the crying, grabbing, and throwing taking place back at base camp. Soon we were actually grateful for our out-of-the-way table location.

There were some good moments for us as a couple and as a family that weekend, but if we were completely honest, we'd have to say there was plenty of misery as well. The crowded lodge room, the half-sick child, the sleep-resistant baby and sleep-deprived parents, and the seemingly endless meals between the kitchen and the storage room were actually pretty easy to leave behind us when the morning came to check out and head for home.

By the time we stopped for lunch, we felt like we might actually survive this familymoon. Because of his ear infection, Caleb had been drinking a lot but eating very little all weekend, so when he asked for a milk shake, we happily consented. We were sure that meant he was feeling better and that the number of stops behind the bushes to point him downwind might even be fewer the rest of the way home.

It turned out to be true that fewer bushes were needed the rest of the way home, but not fewer stops. We were hardly a half hour back up the highway when we heard a terrible series of sounds from the backseat and turned to see Caleb erupting chocolate milk shake all over himself, his brother, and a major portion of the backseat. A terrible odor quickly filled the car, and I pulled off the highway and tumbled out, hoping for a spot that was upwind.

Just when I was thinking things couldn't get worse, I looked back to see flashing blue lights pulling in behind our car. I knew we were at a spot on the interstate where only emergency stopping was allowed, and I found my mind racing to the question of whether or not this stern-looking state trooper would find vomited chocolate milk shake a legitimate emergency.

While the trooper called in our license plate and made sure there weren't any outstanding warrants for us, we continued our relief operation in the backseat. With only a few tissues and fast-food napkins to work with, we were dabbing and mopping the inside of the car and stripping the clothes off our two screaming offspring. Every ten or fifteen seconds I had to step back from the car to catch a fresh breath of car exhaust from the highway before I could bear to stick my head back into the car.

Most healthy families I know wouldn't trade their trips together for anything.

When the state trooper reached our car and snapped off his sunglasses to look in over my shoulder, our backseat was still pretty gruesome. I have a cousin who is a state trooper, and I know they sometimes have to deal with some pretty grizzly crime scenes. But the shocked and repulsed expression on his face as he came upon our own little scene convinced me that this was one of the worst things this particular trooper had happened upon in a long time. Maybe he was a dad himself, or maybe he was just overwhelmed with pity, but his stern, professional look quickly melted into compassion, and he asked if there was any way he could assist us. However, when I told him we were almost finished and would soon be back on the road, he was visibly relieved.

I'm not sure we ever got that smell completely out of the backseat of that car. In fact, that unique fragrance probably cost us a few hundred dollars in trade-in value when we sold it a year or two later. More than showing us the pains and perils of family travel, that fifth anniversary familymoon showed us that traveling together is one of the habits that brings families closer together and gives them memories to enjoy for years to come.

The more your family grows, the easier it is sometimes to just stay home. Packing and preparing to travel as a group can be a hassle. Traveling itself can be expensive. And often it seems like the trip just didn't turn out the way you'd planned. But most healthy families I know wouldn't trade their trips together for anything.

Once when our two older boys were about five and three, we were traveling across country from Illinois to Colorado, and we pulled into a motel somewhere in Nebraska late one night. It took me a while to check in at the front desk because there was a big party going on at the hotel. In fact, it looked like a crazy costume party of some kind. There were crowds of people throughout the lobby, but fortunately, the desk clerk told me there was a side entrance near the elevators that would put us fairly close to our room.

By the time I got back to the car, three-year-old Noah was pretty stir crazy. We contained him across the parking lot, but as soon as he was inside, he was running down the hallway to be the first to press the elevator call button. He didn't realize that the elevator was already on the way down, and just as he pressed the button the elevator doors slid open. Standing in the elevator was a monstrous man wearing some kind of sinister costume that included a gas mask pulled over his head and face.

Noah took one look at that monster, backpedaled until he fell on his bottom, then let out a bloodcurdling scream and ran as fast as he could back in our direction. The costumed man felt horrible and quickly peeled off his mask and dropped to his knees in an effort to show our screaming little boy that he was human and even friendly. But Noah would have none of it. Squeezing my neck for dear life, he continued to scream and cry and look terrified until my wife convinced the sheepish man that the best thing he could do for us was go on his way. It was about two years before Noah would press an elevator button or even walk through its frightening doors without us checking it out first. Ten years after that traumatic event, we still occasionally caution Noah not to get on an elevator until we make sure there's not an alien on it.

Our family could recount literally hundreds of memory-making stories from our travels together over the years. So could Mary and Joseph.

Every year Jesus' parents went to Jerusalem for the Passover festival. When Jesus was twelve years old, they attended the festival as usual. After the celebration was over, they started home to Nazareth, but Jesus stayed behind in Jerusalem. His parents didn't miss him at first, because they assumed he was with friends among the other travelers. But when he didn't show up that evening, they started to look for him among their relatives and friends.

Luke 2:41–45

You don't read a lot about family vacations in the Bible, but I think it might be fair to call this trip to Jerusalem a vacation for Jesus and his parents. The Bible says they traveled to the Passover festival "as usual," and since Jesus was twelve, it was obviously a familiar trip for the family. It would have been natural for several families to travel together during the multiday hike from Nazareth to Jerusalem, and Jesus was obviously independent enough by that age for Mary and Joseph to assume he might be traveling separately with friends.

I imagine "the year Jesus stayed in Jerusalem when he was twelve and we couldn't find him" became part of the travel folklore for Mary and Joseph's family. And it probably wasn't the only story in that folklore.

When a family travels together, bonds are created and memories are made that wouldn't have happened at home. It's worth the time and effort and expense, because some things in life you only experience on the road.

Have you discovered the benefits of purposefully traveling together as a family? Here are some things we've discovered that can make a time like that most meaningful and effective.

Helping Your Family Practice Traveling Together as a Home Team

1. Use Trips to Teach Perspective

Then the LORD told Abram, "Leave your country, your relatives, and your father's house, and go to the land that I will show you. I will cause you to become the father of a great nation. I will bless you and make you famous, and I will make you a blessing to others. I will bless those who bless you and curse those who curse you. All the families of the earth will be blessed through you."

Genesis 12:1–3

All five of the tips in this chapter draw from the example of Abraham and his family. Of course, Abraham wasn't loading his clan into a minivan and filling up on drive-through meals on the way to Walleyworld. But his is one of the first up-close examples in the Bible of a family who is not only on the go but also on the go under God's direction.

When God first told Abram to leave home and go to a new place, he made it clear that he was going to do wonderful things for him and through him. God also gave Abram a new perspective on his life. He would become the father of a great nation, he would be famous, and he would be a blessing to all the families of the earth. Wow. That's a pretty different view than Abram had before the trip.

> One of the things I like best about traveling together as a family is the chance we have to talk about "the big picture"—where each of us is going and how we're doing.

Perspective can be one of the great benefits of traveling together as a family. Our lives at home can be sort of like living among the trees. Traveling can take us up the hill to a view of the forest. When we leave the familiar surroundings of home life, along with most of its possessions and comforts, we are forced to lift our gaze a little and see our lives in a new context. Things are a little less secure and predictable.

We may also notice people more, including our own families, because on a trip they're right there all the time, sometimes for a long period of time. Traveling together gives us opportunities to reconnect and catch up with the people who live in our houses but whose lives and concerns may be blurry to us because their lives are as fast-paced as our own.

One of the things I like best about traveling together as a family is the chance we have to talk about "the big picture"—where each of us is going and how we're doing. That can mean looking back over the past school or work year and reflecting on what we've been through or looking ahead to the challenges the coming year will bring. It can mean solving problems that we left back at home, since we've now placed some time and distance between us and those problems. It can mean setting goals or sharing dreams.

It's also all too easy to bury our faces in a book or electronic toy while we travel together. And certainly those can help pass the time during long trips. But if we will seize teachable moments during a family trip, we can help our families see their lives in a larger context.

I can remember making some major decisions while away on trips. On one trip I decided it was time to propose to Beth. On another trip we decided it was time to move our family across the country. I anticipate a trip in the future where we choose a son's college. Traveling together often provides time for thought, reflection, and discussion with our spouses and families. And it all happens in a context that is outside our normal, sometimes myopic world. Sometimes that's all we need to make some new discoveries.

It's interesting to note that in Genesis 11 Terah, Abram's father, actually left the family's original home in Ur and was heading toward Canaan, the land God would eventually give Abram's descendants. But the Bible says Terah stopped in a place called Haran, where he settled and eventually died. It was after Terah died that God said to Abram, "Let's go." And it wasn't until Abram actually arrived in Canaan that God told him, "This is it—this is the land I'll give your offspring."

It's as if there are certain things about life that we can't see clearly from just one point of reference. Being away from home, and with our families, often gives us a new perspective on life and its challenges and opportunities. But we have to lift our eyes and look for that new perspective. Trips are the perfect opportunity to help our families do just that.

2. Plan Purposeful Family Journeys

Traveling through Canaan, they came to a place near Shechem and set up camp beside the oak at Moreh. At that time, the area was inhabited by Canaanites.

Then the LORD appeared to Abram and said, "I am going to give this land to your offspring." And Abram built an altar there to commemorate the LORD's visit.

Genesis 12:6–7

Sometimes family trips are just necessary. It's Christmastime or someone's graduating or getting married, and we just need to load up and go. Those can be meaningful times together, even if they're to familiar places with familiar people.

In addition, it can be a great experience for our families to plan trips together that take us to new places, perhaps for new purposes. We may want to climb a fourteen-thousand-foot mountain together or go deep-sea fishing for the first time. We may want to see historic places or famously beautiful places. We may want to see Congress in session or walk where Jesus walked.

The benefits of a planned, purposeful vacation or trip are that we can work together on it and that it can be an expression of our families' own interests or dreams. For weeks, months, or even years in advance, we can anticipate it and prepare for it. Sometimes that's even the best part.

Have you ever been asked, "If your house were burning down and you could only rescue one possession, what would it be?" In nearly every setting where I've heard that question posed, family photo albums are frequently mentioned as the most valued possession. When I've asked why that photo album is so valued, I've often discovered that the main subject of those photos is special family trips.

Abram's trip with his family to Canaan was certainly purposeful. He went not only to obey God but also to find his family's future. Then, as his family traveled through Canaan, God fulfilled the purpose of the trip and showed Abram the place where his family's future would be rooted. The land Abram was given extended farther than his eyes could see. But the place where God appeared and delivered his promise was a very specific place—near Shechem and beside a particular oak tree. In effect, Abram took a snapshot. He built an altar and marked the place so he and his family would be able to remember where God made this significant promise and fulfilled the purpose for their journey and their future.

Several years ago I took my wife and family back to the campus where I attended college for one year—the most spiritually rebellious year of my life. Oh, we also went to an amusement park for the kids and to a conference I needed to attend, but long before we left home I had planned what this trip was about. As we walked onto that campus, I guided them to a specific footbridge over a little stream. It was there that as a college freshman I had finally stopped running from God and turned back to give him my life.

Our children were too young to fully comprehend the significance of the place, and if you asked them today, they'd find it easier to remember the amusement park than the footbridge. What my wife remembers, though, is my lying down on that footbridge and hanging over its side to nail a little wooden sign that read, "Jesus." It had been given to me by the students in my youth group—the one I started serving as a youth minister the year after I transferred from this college. And it was now my own private altar that reminded me of God's faithfulness to me in that place.

Before we left we took a couple of snapshots that commemorated the purpose of our journey. But for me, the trip itself was one of those snapshots that commemorated God's purpose in my life's journey. He had brought me to that significant place for a purpose. And now I brought my family there to thank him for how he had led me since I left that place with him as my guide.

Where are the purposeful journeys your family needs to plan? Where will you look for your future or commemorate God's faithfulness in your past? When you look back at the snapshots, you'll be grateful for every purposeful family journey you planned.

3. Make Room for Spontaneous Trips

Later on God tested Abraham's faith and obedience. "Abraham!" God called.

"Yes," he replied. "Here I am."

"Take your son, your only son—yes, Isaac, whom you love so much—and go to the land of Moriah. Sacrifice him there as a burnt offering on one of the mountains, which I will point out to you."

The next morning Abraham got up early. He saddled his donkey and took two of his servants with him, along with his son Isaac. Then he chopped wood to build a fire for a burnt offering and set out for the place where God had told him to go.

Genesis 22:1–3

Family trips usually require some planning, packing, and purchasing, and it's no fun to be five hundred miles from home and realize you forgot something important. But don't underestimate the potential of occasional spontaneous trips, whether it's a day trip for an unexpected adventure or an overnight trip to just get away or to talk about something important.

Planned trips can be full of anticipation, but spontaneous trips can be full of adrenaline. "Where are we going? Why didn't you tell me? When will we be back?" The atmosphere of surprise can create a climate for faith and trust. And faith and trust are relationship builders.

> **Planned trips can be full of anticipation, but spontaneous trips can be full of adrenaline.**

Abraham had listened to God, obeyed God, and followed God enough to trust him when he unexpectedly asked Abraham to take his son Isaac to the mountains. There was more than one child trusting his father on that excursion. But as Abraham trusted God and Isaac trusted Abraham, they had a wonderful, life-changing experience together. Hundreds and hundreds of years before Jesus would die on a cross for their sin, Abraham and Isaac saw a picture of that miraculous provision. And their family photo album, recorded in Genesis 22, continues to encourage us today. Spontaneous trips are often worth the effort and the surprise and the trust required.

Years ago Beth and I had an opportunity to go on a cruise in the Caribbean. We hadn't been gone long before the ship was abuzz about one poor passenger whose luggage had been lost by the airline that brought him to Miami, our departure port. They promised to have it delivered to him at our next port, but as day after day and port after port went by, his luggage didn't arrive.

The most surprising thing to us was that his misfortune didn't seem to affect his attitude or enjoyment of the cruise at all. In fact, he was having a ball. The cruise line was so sympathetic that they offered him free clothes from the gift shop. Fellow passengers he had never met before generously shared anything he might need, from tanning lotion to sunglasses. While everyone dressed nicely for dinner, he was allowed to wear shorts and a flowered shirt.

In short, he was the most popular, pampered guy on the ship. His trip wasn't what he had planned. It was much better than that.

Proverbs 16:9 says, "In his heart a man plans his course, but the LORD determines his steps" (NIV). There's something very fun about being "ready to roll" when God's surprises come along and we respond with faith. After all, Jesus walked up to Andrew and Peter, and then James and John, and simply said, "Come, follow me . . ." (Matt. 4:19). Planning a trip or two where your family has to just trust you and enjoy being together might give you the snapshot of a lifetime.

4. Give Everyone His or Her Own Space

> Then Abram talked it over with Lot. "This arguing between our herdsmen has got to stop," he said. "After all, we are close relatives! I'll tell you what we'll do. Take your choice of any section of the land you want, and we will separate. If you want that area over there, then I'll stay here. If you want to stay in this area, then I'll move on to another place."
>
> Genesis 13:8–9

Whether a trip is planned or spontaneous, near or far, by plane, train, or automobile, it's bound to create some family tensions. Unless we're like Noah in the Bible and our mode of transportation is bigger than our house, travel, almost by definition, pushes the family into closer proximity and less personal space. It was true for Abraham and Lot, and it's worth thinking about and planning for if we don't want our families to dread traveling together rather than enjoying it.

Close proximity is actually one of the benefits of family trips. Trips can pull everyone out of their rooms or basements or cars or friends' houses or offices and put them together for a while where they can talk and eat and plan and dream together.

But there are certain things we can do as we travel that make being so close more enjoyable. For example, our family has a series of Christian tapes and CDs that, somewhat amazingly, we all like to listen to in the car. We also have several games we play in the car, some that come out of a box and some that use the landscape around us as we drive. One of the most beneficial things we can do for our families as we travel is to come up with creative, interesting ways to play together and interact as we drive. Headphones and books are sometimes a welcome relief, but every minute we spend truly relating as a family is time to be cherished.

> **One of the most beneficial things we can do for our families as we travel is to come up with creative, interesting ways to play together and interact as we drive.**

In addition to planning activities that draw the family together, we're wise if we take steps to allow everyone a reasonable amount of personal space when the family travels together. Seat assignments, boundaries, and taking turns can help. In our family, we ask each of our guys to pack a backpack of stuff they like to do as we travel, and that luggage has to fit with them wherever they sit as we travel.

Occasionally, little things like that can make weary travelers feel a little more at home as they travel abroad. The goal is to pull the home team together in the unusually close way that travel allows, while not crowding them together physically or emotionally in a way that feels smothering.

5. Mix Adventure and Tradition in Your Travels

Abraham was now a very old man, and the Lord had blessed him in every way. One day Abraham said to the man in charge of his household, who was his oldest servant, "Swear by the LORD, the God of heaven and earth, that you will not let my son marry one of these local Canaanite women. Go instead to my homeland, to my relatives, and find a wife there for my son Isaac."

Genesis 24:1–4

By the time Abraham was an old man, he was pretty well traveled. He was no doubt grateful for the new home God had brought him and his family. But he also recognized that his son Isaac needed a wife who shared his faith and values. So he sent his servant on—you guessed it—another trip. This time instead of going forward to find his future in a new land, he sent his servant back to the place of his roots.

> **It is good to travel together with our families to places that both embrace future adventure and honor past tradition.**

Our family has found great satisfaction in both these kinds of trips—the ones that lead forward to unknown adventure and the ones that lead back to roots and tradition. Adventure travel is where we advance into new frontiers and share risks that help us grow. Tradition travel is where we retreat to familiar people and places and share the values that help us stay grounded.

We seem to do most of our adventure travel during the summer, when time and weather allow us freedom to be outdoors. We do tradition traveling at various times, but especially during holidays, when families seem most able to reunite around that which binds them together.

My simple point here is to encourage families to embrace both kinds of travel together. We mustn't be so hungry for adventure and the future that we don't return to the places that commemorate our values and God's faithfulness to us in the past. But we also shouldn't be so shackled to tradition that all our travel returns us to the same familiar places. It is good to travel together with our families to places that both embrace future adventure and honor past tradition.

After Abraham instructed his servant to go back to the family's homeland and find a wife for Isaac, the servant asked what he should do if the wife God led him to for Isaac was unwilling to come back with him to Canaan. Abraham was very direct—Isaac was not to go back. God had made it clear that his future was in the land to which God had led them years ago. Fortunately, Abraham's servant was led to a young woman named Rebekah, who was willing to bring the values and faith of Abraham's homeland to the future adventure of Isaac's journey.

As your home team practices traveling together, you will gain perspective and make memories. You will take your family to places that will stretch them and help them grow and to places that will anchor them and keep them rooted. Abraham's family found great blessing in traveling together and trusting God as he guided them. Our families can too.

Please *Do* Try This at Home

1. Start planning your family's next trip that will have a special purpose beyond visiting family or going to a conference. What kind of a trip would capture the imagination of your whole family and get them excited about preparing for it? Also plan meaningful activities or "altars" during the trip that commemorate the trip's significance and point to God's faithfulness.
2. Plan a trip with your family to one or more of the significant places in your life. It may be the church where you were baptized or the place where you and your spouse first met. That may be a major cross-country trip or a drive across town some Saturday.

7

Sharing the Pain

The Practice of Hurting Together

Adopting a puppy into our family wasn't exactly an impulse decision, but it also wasn't a decision to which we applied our very best thinking. After several weekends of "shopping" at local Humane Society locations and rescue centers, we finally brought home a darling little black puppy with brown markings and named him Sammy (after Sammy Sosa, the Chicago Cubs slugger who was having a great year).

That first week was the only time we used the word *darling* to describe Sammy. While he had many good qualities, he was a mutt whose precise behavior patterns were hard to predict. The lady from the adoption center vowed that he would only reach thirty-five or forty pounds, which was the size pet we were seeking. The veterinarian there on-site even said she thought she could see a little Chihuahua in the shape of his head. These two ladies, of course, were in the business of finding homes for puppies.

The lady at the pet supply store was a little more transparent with us. "Oh, a little rottie!" she exclaimed, when we asked her to help us select some supplies for the new little guy at our house.

"Rotting?" I said, fearful that she had recognized some deteriorative fungus condition that the vet hadn't told us about.

"No, rottie," she repeated. "Rottweiler!"

My wife turned to me. "Rottweiler?" she repeated. "Isn't that a . . . a large dog?" I rushed over to the book section of the pet supply store and found a dog guidebook with pictures and descriptions. Even the photograph of the rottweiler startled—OK, scared—me a little. But what scared me even more was the description that said it wasn't unusual for "rotties" to be 110 to 120 pounds when full grown.

When the lady at the pet supply store realized we weren't *trying* to adopt a large dog, she quickly joined in on the adoption center's conspiracy. "Oh, I just mean he has some of those same colors," she recovered quickly. "This puppy has a lot of different breeds in him, and it wouldn't surprise me if he stays much smaller than that."

Well, depending on your definition of *much*, I guess she was right. Sammy topped the scales a few months later at seventy pounds, and it was all any of us could do to contain him on a leash. He remained 110 percent puppy in spite of his size, and his first-year exploits included chewing a hole in the wall of our kitchen and breaking my mother-in-law's shoulder by dragging her down a hill. A neighbor once asked me what kind of dog he was, and without thinking I simply replied, "Evil."

Of course, Sammy wasn't evil. He was just a large, strong puppy with attention deficit disorder. And we learned to live with it. But the pain he brought us continued to eclipse the pleasure.

One morning my wife called me at the office. "Something's happened," she began, and my mind raced to imagine the worst. Aging parents, school bus accidents, home invasions, and car wrecks all darted through my mind before she could continue. "Sammy's been hit by a car."

Forgive me, dog lovers, for my relieved, pleasantly surprised tone of voice as I answered almost with glee, "Oh! How about that!" Then, hearing my heartless reflex response out loud, I quickly said, "I mean, oh . . . uh . . . that's awful . . . uh . . . what happened?"

Beth explained that while waiting for the school bus with our kids out in front of the house, stronger-than-the-average-human Sammy had bolted loose to chase an oncoming car. It had been a deflecting blow, but Sammy's

> **Our boys had to get on a school bus full of kids that morning, not knowing whether their buddy Sammy would live or die.**

rear leg appeared to be broken, and it was unclear whether he had suffered internal injuries. Our boys had to get on a school bus full of kids that morning, not knowing whether their buddy Sammy would live or die.

The next phone call I received from Beth was in some ways more painful to me than the first. Sammy would live. His leg was broken, and not very cleanly. Our two options—expensive and very expensive—were a splint that probably wouldn't do much good with an active puppy like Sammy or surgery, complete with pins, medicines, follow-up visits, and X rays.

Well, Sammy had taken some big bites in his short life but none as big as the one he now threatened to take out of my bank account. With as much tact as I could muster, I made compelling, persuasive arguments for both splints and euthanasia. But the vet had already been more persuasive with Beth, and she was the one standing there looking at a pitiful, lame puppy. The decision was painful but not that difficult. Sammy would have surgery.

That night during our family devotions, Sammy was the subject. We had all been through an emotional wringer that day. Still, I began with a pretty harsh statement. "Guys, I need you to understand that Sammy on his own has no real value."

Afraid that I had changed my mind about Sammy's surgery, our sons desperately and creatively argued that Sammy had intrinsic value.

"We paid sixty dollars for him—he's worth that!" Ethan offered.

"No, that sixty dollars was for his shots and neutering," I replied firmly. "It was so he could be a responsible member of society, a role that he obviously has not yet learned. No, Sammy was free. And now he has become very costly."

"We could get him a job. He could work to pay us back!" Noah offered.

"Doing what?" Beth laughed out loud.

Realizing the lack of marketable skills his overgrown puppy possessed, Noah grasped for the absurd. "I don't know—he's strong—he could pull sticks around or something and help people clean up their yards."

Instead of ridiculing Noah for his well-intentioned idea, we just paused for a minute to let that image sink in—the image of this crazed, uncontainable puppy dragging a stack of sticks around a yard in a manner that somehow merited a paycheck. Noah chuckled sheepishly and said, "I guess not," and we moved on.

"Guys," I continued, "there's no way around it. Sammy has no value of his own. No one would buy him from us. No one would hire him. We'd be fortunate to find someone who would take him off our hands for free. And today he's gone beyond simple worthlessness—he's become extremely costly. We could buy a decent used car or some new furniture for what his surgery will cost. And after he's mended and healed, he's likely to be just as rebellious and wild as he was before. He'll still do pretty much whatever he wants, limited only by whatever discipline we bring into his life."

I was painting a pretty harsh, dim picture of the beloved family pet, and the faces of my family were starting to cloud up. This was the teachable moment, the time to make the point.

"But you know what?" I continued. The word *but* seemed to offer hope, and their downcast faces looked up. "Today, on this day when Sammy proved himself to be most costly, today we have given him great value. We have chosen of our own free will to pay a high price for his healing and restoration to our family. We have paid more for him than if he were purebred. Today we have chosen to love him with a love he'll never understand and to pay a price he can never repay. It's not anything in Sammy that gives him that value. It's something in us. When Sammy was most helpless and hopeless, we chose to give him our compassion and mercy. Today Sammy has great value, because he has received from us great love that required great sacrifice."

It was a quiet moment, one filled with reflection and a little puzzlement, as they processed what I was saying.

"But do you know what's even more amazing to me than that?" I continued. I think they were still kind of puzzled about why I was making such a sermon out of this event, but they were patient in waiting for my point, because they understood that I myself was working through the pain of paying a pretty big veterinary bill. "What's more amazing than that is that what we just did for Sammy is what God has done for us."

I turned to Romans 5 and started reading:

When we were utterly helpless, Christ came at just the right time and died for us sinners. Now, no one is likely to die for a good person, though someone might be willing to die for a person who is especially good. But God showed his great love for us by sending Christ to die for us while we were still sinners.

Romans 5:6–8

"Guys," I continued, "you have a hard time seeing Sammy as worthless because you have chosen to love him. And the Bible says that even though you and I were selfish and rebellious, God chose to love us and give us the sacrifice of his own Son, Jesus. Today we hurt over Sammy's recklessness that led to his helplessness, and that hurt led us to compassion and mercy that came from love. God feels that same way about us."

I may not have said it quite perfectly that night, but our family got it. Somehow we had walked through the trauma and pain and frustration and expense of that day and come out the other side with an emotional bond and a glimpse of God that made us stronger and more united.

For our family, the day Sammy got hit by the car was one of those unexpected opportunities that come with pain. We all suffered the trauma of Sammy's injury. Our kids suffered the daylong anguish of not knowing whether he was going to live or die. Beth suffered the guilt of being the one whose hand had let go of the leash. And while I empathized with all of the above, my additional pain came from the hundreds of dollars that suddenly left us without even bothering to take the dog with them.

God says that pain is full of opportunity.

Dear brothers and sisters, whenever trouble comes your way, let it be an opportunity for joy. For when your faith is tested, your endurance has a chance to grow. So let it grow, for when your endurance is fully developed, you will be strong in character and ready for anything.

James 1:2–4

While times of significant hurt or pain are often unpredictable, they are among the best opportunities in life to strengthen and grow a Christian family. The key is in developing the habit of hurting together. And that means both preparing our families for life's inevitable difficulties and then choosing to respond with Christ-like character under the pressure of those difficulties.

Have you discovered the benefits of learning to hurt together as a family? Here are some things we've discovered that can make a time like that most meaningful and effective.

Helping Your Family Practice Hurting Together as a Home Team

1. During the Good Times, Remind Your Family That There Will Be Bad Times

I have told you all this so that you may have peace in me. Here on earth you will have many trials and sorrows. But take heart, because I have overcome the world.

John 16:33

Many times pain can drive wedges in families rather than unify and strengthen them. Why? Because truly painful times often come suddenly and unexpectedly. If we saw them coming, we could do more to avoid them.

Jesus said that here on earth we *will* (not *may*) have many trials and sorrows. James wrote *whenever* trouble comes your way (James 1:2), not *if* trouble comes your way. In

> **Even if our families have been blessed with few traumas and deep hurts, they should understand that they're not immune to difficulty.**

other words, trouble is unavoidable in this life. That's why it's important for our families to talk about the inevitability of tough times and to practice our response to them during minor hurts. Even if our families have been blessed with few traumas and deep hurts, they should understand that they're not immune to difficulty. The safety and security of good times can be an important time to prepare for the not-so-good times.

The church where my dad was a pastor during the years I was growing up had a large number of elderly people. In the nine years we served there, he performed over two hundred funerals. While I didn't have a close relationship with most of those people, my dad routinely took me with him to the funeral home during evening visitation times. Years later he told me that he and my mom intentionally did that so that we kids would be able to observe death and funeral homes and the grieving process in a Christian context. At the same time, they were helping us understand and prepare for the experience of death when it hit closer to home. When those times came we were a little more prepared.

It's also important to prepare our families for troubled times with very practical understandings of God's Word. Knowing what God says about facing trials or sorrows before they actually happen can help our families more readily find the peace Jesus promised us in him. The Bible says, "As pressure and stress bear down on me, I find joy in your commands" (Ps. 119:143).

As our own children grew old enough to understand and be concerned about death, we had an opportunity to take our oldest son to the funeral visitation of a friend and former Sunday school teacher. Before leaving for the funeral, we reviewed what the Bible says about death, that Christians who die are "away from the body and at home with the Lord" (2 Cor. 5:8 NIV). Our friend, we explained, was already in heaven with Jesus, but what we were going to see was only his body, and later they would bury his body.

We didn't stay long at the funeral visitation, and as we left we asked our son what he thought. His only question puzzled us at first. "Why do they have to cut your legs off when you die?" he asked innocently. We assured him that was not the case, and then we realized he was referring to the fact that the casket revealed the man's body only from the waist up.

"His legs were there, son, they were just covered up by the bottom of the casket box he was lying in," I explained.

"That's what I thought," he replied, looking puzzled. "But when you said the man was in heaven but they would bury his bottom, I figured they must have to cut off the legs to get to his bottom."

Once we got past that initial misunderstanding about the difference between burying someone's body and burying his bottom, our discussion went much more smoothly. The practical explanation from God's Word—that death separates the eternal person from the temporary human body but that the person goes to heaven if he or she knows Jesus—had been clearly illustrated. A few years later when our son said good-bye to his grandpa, he was able to process his grief in the context of what he knew to be true from God's Word.

2. Shoulder Others' Pain in Prayer as a Family

Confess your sins to each other and pray for each other so that you may be healed. The earnest prayer of a righteous person has great power and wonderful results.

James 5:16

The apostle James encouraged the early church to openly share their needs and even their sins with one another. He knew that God chooses to use intercessory prayer not only to bring healing to those in need but also to build the faith of those who pray. When you see that God answers your prayers for the needs of others, you can't help but trust him a little more with your own needs.

I'm amazed sometimes when our family sits down for a family devotion time and can't seem to think of many prayer needs. The good thing about that is that we are truly blessed by God. The bad thing about it is that we can feel so independent and self-sufficient that we don't rely enough on God or ask him to do more than he's already doing.

But even when we don't think of much to pray about for ourselves, we always seem to have plenty to pray about, because we intercede for our extended family, our church, our friends, and sometimes people we've just heard about in the news. Most people don't have to go very far outside their own lives to find hurt and need in the lives of others.

> **Intercession is a powerful way for families to learn to hurt together during a time when their vision isn't blurred by their own pain.**

Intercession is a powerful way for families to learn to hurt together during a time when their vision isn't blurred by their own pain. As we empathize and come before God with the needs of others, we are drawn together and prepared to help. We also learn how to think about pain during a time when we can be more objective and when we can have a clearer view of God's overarching principles and purposes.

Jesus said we are even to pray for those who mistreat us (Luke 6:28). If you want to have an interesting family devotion sometime, ask your family to make a list of the people who are causing them the most frustration or pain. Then focus your prayer time on those people and their needs. It really is true that "hurt people hurt people," and the more you pray for those who are mistreating you, the more likely you are to understand the origins of their hurtful behavior.

So when things are going well for your family, praying for the hurts of others will train you to look for God's perspective on trials and adversities. When your family is going through hurt of your own, praying for those who may be causing or contributing to the hurt will take your focus off yourselves and may even lead to a solution with the persons contributing to your pain.

3. Learn from Your Hurts as a Family—Don't Ask Why, Ask What

So if you are suffering according to God's will, keep on doing what is right, and trust yourself to the God who made you, for he will never fail you.

1 Peter 4:19

When hurt hits your family hard, the most natural question to ask is, why? Stories in the Bible illustrate this over and over, but none illustrate it more painstakingly than the book of Job. God is patient with Job until he starts asking why. Then God issues a stern reminder that his motive and character are not to be questioned. The right question is not if we can understand all God's ways and reasons for acting as he does, but if we will trust him and obey him no matter what. As my pastor father once said in a sermon I'll always remember, "The big question posed by the book of Job is not, Why does a man suffer? The big question in the book of Job is, Why does a man serve God?"

One of the most important things to teach our families as they grow together by hurting together is not to question God's motive or character by asking why but to seek

God's direction by asking what. Not "God, why did you let Dad lose his job?" but "God, what new direction do you want us to go in now that Dad's job will change?" Not "God, why did you let Grandpa die?" but "God, what kind of life without Grandpa will make our reunion with him the most joyful?"

When we teach our families to ask the "what" question instead of the "why" question, we teach them that life's troubles are not God's clenched fist of wrath but rather his open hand of opportunity and guidance. Then even the hurtful experiences of life can draw us closer to God for guidance and character development and closer to one another for support and strength.

The Bible teaches again and again that trusting and obeying God during difficult times pleases him immensely and also develops and perfects our character so that we become more and more like Christ. Peter says there are actually times when our suffering is according to God's will. What should we do when that happens? Resent God and ask him to stop? No, Peter says we should keep on doing what is right and trust God to accomplish what he wants to do in our lives, even if we don't understand why.

In the Old Testament (see Deut. 8:2), we see that God's people are given difficulty to prove what's really in their hearts. The psalmist writes that it was actually good that he was "afflicted" (Ps. 119:71 NIV) because it led him to learn God's decrees. Paul writes to the Roman church that they could rejoice in their sufferings because those sufferings could produce perseverance, character, and hope (Rom. 5:3–5). And the writer of the Epistle to the Hebrews reminds us that hardship is often the loving discipline of our heavenly Dad (Heb. 12:7–11).

If our families learn to shake an angry fist at God and ask why, our hurt will only deepen and our frustration will only increase. But as we teach our families to look for God's purposes in pain, we'll find their faith will be stretched and their characters will mature to increasingly imitate Christ.

4. Consistently Emphasize God's Sovereignty

As far as I am concerned, God turned into good what you meant for evil. He brought me to the high position I have today so I could save the lives of many people.

Genesis 50:20

I have discovered that one of the most comforting sentences I can offer to others during times of great pain or loss is simply this: God is not surprised by this, and it's not outside his control. And when my family has faced times of pain or fear, I have watched those same words bring visible relief and security to their faces.

Joseph had endured a life of betrayal, false accusation, imprisonment, abandonment, and many other hurts, all because of the jealousy and hateful treatment of his older brothers. Yet his teachable spirit allowed him to see God's hand in all these things and to trust that no event in his life was outside God's control. Because he trusted in God's sovereignty, he persevered and escaped not only the temporary trials but also the lifelong prison of anger and bitterness that could so easily have been his.

God's sovereignty is a truth that is most effective in helping our families through hurtful times when we have consistently taught it and reinforced it before those times come along. When we study the Bible, we talk about God's unthwartable plan of redemption and his ultimate victory over Satan and sin. When we see unrest in the Middle East on the evening news, we talk about the miraculous way God has preserved Israel for his ultimate purposes. When we pray for others, we pray not exclusively for their comfort or well-being but for their faithfulness and maturing and for God's ultimate purposes to be accomplished in their lives.

When our families are confronted with their own hurt, they can stand firm on the foundational truth that God's knowledge, power, presence, and love are unquestionable and inexhaustible. In God's sovereignty we can find the security and confidence we need to endure pain and even grow stronger through it.

5. Lead Your Family to Express Genuine Gratitude When Things Are Good

O God, you have taught me from my earliest childhood,
    and I have constantly told others about the wonderful
    things you do.
Now that I am old and gray,
    do not abandon me, O God.
Let me proclaim your power to this new generation,
    your mighty miracles to all who come after me.

Your righteousness, O God, reaches to the highest heavens.
    You have done such wonderful things.
    Who can compare with you, O God?

Psalm 71:17–19

Many families have a Thanksgiving tradition of going around the table and having family members list the things for which they're most grateful. That's actually a great exercise to do monthly or even weekly rather than annually. One of the best ways to help your family cope with the stresses and insecurities of hurtful times is to build up an awareness and appreciation for the blessings that are present during normal times.

Of course, this needs to include more than just material blessings. Being intentionally grateful for things like health and safety communicates to your family (and to God!) that these are not things you take for granted. And the times when you empathize with and pray for people who are not currently enjoying health or safety are very appropriate times to thank God for that which he provides most of the time.

The good things for which you lead your family to express gratitude should also include gifts and talents, accomplishments, family and national heritage, friendships, your church family, and personal freedoms. These are the things that tend to endure and prevail through hurtful times, and counting these blessings can give your family a reservoir to draw from when going through the drought of personal hurts.

The most important subjects of our gratitude when things are good should be the things that nothing can take away, not even death. Salvation, God's sovereignty, God's trustworthiness and perfect character, the hope of heaven and eternity with God where every tear will be wiped away—these are the things that can become our focus when walking through life's darkest valleys and deepest hurts. The first couple of times you lead your family through thoughts of deep gratitude for salvation or for God's abiding goodness, they may think you're just being sentimental. But if you as a parent consistently return to that gratitude and with heartfelt humility express how lost and hopeless you were before God rescued you, then your family will, over time, develop that same appreciation that you are modeling. And even on that day when death separates you from them, you can leave with the comfort and hope that the good times ultimately prevail.

Please *Do* Try This at Home

1. This week find some time to talk with your family about the most painful times you've been through together. Ask each family member what he or she learned about your family and about God during that

experience. Then speculate with them what kinds of trouble your family might face in the future. (Don't borrow trouble or allow this to create anxiety about the future. Emphasize that these things may or may not happen but that, whatever happens, it doesn't jeopardize God's sovereignty or your family's love and commitment to one another.) Then determine together the best way to respond to that trouble. This isn't unlike preparing for a fire or tornado at your house! The preparedness could come in handy. It may also make your family feel more empathetic toward others and even feel some relief that they are somewhat prepared to deal with that trouble—but don't have to yet!

2. If you don't have one already, start a family prayer list of the people you know who are in trouble or going through difficulty right now. In addition to praying for them by name as a family, talk about specific things for which you can petition God on their behalf. In addition to relief from the trouble or pain, pray for things like character strengthening, faithfulness, and a deeper walk with God.

3. Identify one family, perhaps in your church or neighborhood, who is going through a difficult time or is hurting deeply. It may be someone who is seriously ill, unemployed, or persevering through a difficult transition of some kind. Brainstorm with your family specific actions you could take that would encourage and support that family without embarrassing them. Make a plan to implement your best idea.

8

Boarding the Bus

The Practice of Changing Together

As I sat down on the big front step of our house, I remembered to give the concrete a quick brush to help keep my suit pants clean. Countless times before, I had plopped down in that same spot to put on my tennis shoes for a game of driveway basketball or backyard baseball with my two preschool sons.

But I no longer had two preschool sons. My oldest son was beginning kindergarten. In just a few moments, Caleb would climb onto a big yellow bus and travel two miles out of our reach.

Caleb had been unusually quiet for the past couple of days and didn't really want to talk about school at all. As long as kindergarten was a far-off, future event, it had sounded fine to him. Throughout the summer we had talked about how fun and exciting school would be, and if Caleb felt anxiety then, he didn't show it. But "the day after tomorrow" and then "tomorrow" were time periods he understood a little better.

Part of what made his apparent anxiety hard for me to understand is that I don't remember kindergarten being a big deal. I'm a fairly independent, just-deal-with-it type of guy who isn't particularly upset by change and doesn't spend a lot of time fretting about it. Caleb is more like his mother—sensitive, tenderhearted, and cautious about change. In fact, when Beth and I were dating, I learned the hard way that we had very different sensitivity levels. As a gag, I once hung her love-worn childhood teddy bear from the ceiling and left a suicide note. She didn't laugh when she discovered it, and that didn't necessarily surprise me. But when she walked over to "Bear Bear" and tenderly untied him without saying a word, I knew I had missed the mark badly in trying to amuse her. Then when she turned and I saw the tear running down her cheek, I knew I had also grossly underestimated the tenderness of her heart.

That Beth passed on that tender heart to Caleb was quite evident from a very early age, and it was now making this first day of kindergarten an especially emotional one. Hearing them come out the front door behind me, I turned to a fairly pitiable sight. Instead of wearing any of his new school clothes, Caleb had chosen his favorite summer play shirt—the one that had been sewn up three or four times yet still had a threadbare run down the front. I looked up from his shirt to my wife's teary eyes, but the quick shake of her head told me not to ask about his tattered choice.

Caleb came slithering through the door but continued to hold on to the doorknob as if he didn't want to lose this last grasp of his familiar home. Then he shyly buried his face in the screen. He's not supposed to lean on the screen like that—I've told him dozens of times. But I restrained myself from correcting him.

Beth and I chatted with deliberate, forced enthusiasm about how exciting it would be to ride the bus and what fun things they would probably do at kindergarten. We were obviously trying to convince ourselves as well as our door-clutching son. Just the night before, Beth had fretted over the fruit snack Caleb was supposed to bring to school each day. Bananas were the only fruit he was interested in bringing, and it had suddenly occurred to Beth that she had always peeled his bananas for him.

In a panic, she gave him a crash course on banana preparation, focusing particularly on how to peel the hard, rubbery kind that bend instead of snapping at the top. Our oversight had clearly rattled Beth, who now wondered how many other vacuums we had negligently left in Caleb's young life. Now as she stole a glance away from our conversation to our turtlelike son, she stopped short and swallowed hard. I looked back to see Caleb quietly crying, his face still buried in the screen door.

It was more than Beth could bear. She turned quickly back into the house to retrieve a tissue, and I knelt in my suit pants beside him. Everything inside me wanted to say that he didn't have to go to that first day of school, or that I'd go with him, or that his mother would drive him to school and stay there with him for the first two or three years until he got used to it.

> **Everything inside me wanted to say that he didn't have to go to that first day of school, or that I'd go with him, or that his mother would drive him to school and stay there with him for the first two or three years until he got used to it.**

At the same time, I knew that was unrealistic and unwise and that my role in this situation was not primarily protection or even empathy but empowerment. So I talked to him about my first day of kindergarten and how it was more fun than I had even imagined. I talked about the fun things he and I would do together that night when I got home. And I hugged him until the shoulder of my freshly pressed shirt was soaked with his tears.

But none of it seemed to work. His mother came back with her handful of tissues and Caleb's four-year-old brother, Noah, who had just awakened. Sleepy and a little disoriented, Noah sat there on the front step with us and watched the tears flow for a few minutes. Eventually his little bottom lip pushed out too, and he started talking about how it wasn't going to be any fun without Caleb there to play with. Soon I had three in tears. My family was falling apart emotionally, and I felt powerless to help.

None of us was prepared for what happened next. Perhaps it was the tightness of my throat from choking back my own tears. Perhaps it was the discomfort of kneeling next to my crying son. Perhaps it was the nutritious toaster pastry I had just finished. I let out a healthy, resonating, man-sized belch. And somehow that which brought relief to my own distraught stomach that morning also brought relief to our family crisis. Everyone stopped short in their sobbing for just a moment. Then the laughter broke loose.

Now, in case you don't recall, ages four and five are ideal ages to be amused by any kind of bodily noise, and the louder the noise, the better. Fueled, I suppose, by the tension of the moment, my two boys got the giggles. So I seized the opportunity. I pled with Caleb not to tell the kids on the bus that his dad made noises like that. I asked him to *please* not tell the kids in his kindergarten class that Daddy produced foul, belchy burps. I dropped to my knees again and *begged* him to keep my secret from his new teacher. And the more I hammed it up, the louder we all laughed—even Beth, who's normally pretty intolerant of my amusing bodily noises.

Suddenly the bus was there. With no time to transition from silliness back to sobbing, Caleb grabbed his bag and headed for the bus. In fact, we had to hurry to keep up with him. The doors to the bus swung open, and the friendliest, kindest bus driver we ever could have hoped for said good morning and called Caleb by name. By name! Beth told me later that the driver had actually come by the day before to practice the route and meet as many of the kids as possible. She knew that would make it easier on everyone. This impressive, capable bus driver helped Caleb to a seat right in the front row, said something cordial and reassuring to Beth and me, and then closed the big swinging doors. From the moment he left the giggles of the front porch, Caleb never looked back.

After the bus pulled away, we were left to deal with real separation, and in many ways it was even harder than anticipated separation. But we reminded ourselves that Caleb was ready for this new step. We affirmed our belief that where he was going would be good for him, even better than staying home. We assured ourselves that he was in very good hands. And we were very, very thankful for the world's best bus driver.

As I drove to work that morning, I pictured little Caleb on the big bus. I pictured him being herded along with twenty other kindergarten sheep into a big room full of new people and new rules. I pictured him carefully peeling his own banana and wondering as he chewed it why he had to leave the security of his own home to eat fruit with kids he didn't know. And there in the car by myself, I found my own tears starting to flow.

This was a new experience for me as a father. It wasn't the first time Caleb had to do something he didn't want to do or the first time he had to step outside his comfort zone. It certainly wasn't the first time we as his parents had required discipline or obedience from him. But it was the first time he was required to go through some major

> **While I was the empowering father on the front step, I'd felt the need to be upbeat, strong, and confident. Now, as a child of God with my own fears and tears, I needed the same assurances from my Father in heaven.**

change based on the outside world's expectations rather than just his parents'. Society and the school system demanded that he start kindergarten. And we couldn't just decide that if Monday didn't go well, he didn't have to go back Tuesday. He was doing what needed to be done, and all of us knew that meant school.

I turned to God in prayer, asking him to protect and comfort my son. While I was the empowering father on the front step, I'd felt the need to be upbeat, strong, and confident. Now, as a child of God with my own fears and tears, I needed the same assurances from my Father in heaven.

In the quiet moments that followed, I found myself reflecting on what God knew about sending a son into a hostile world. Had there been an event like this for God before time began? Wasn't there some kind of moment when he looked upon his own dear Son and saw swaddling clothes instead of majestic robes? Didn't he more or less watch from heaven's front step as Jesus left to do what had to be done and what only he could do? Was the heartache of change and separation infinitely larger for a heavenly Father than an earthly father?

I realized then that there was a good reason why my second first day of school had been so heart wrenching. I had just experienced a faint reflection of what God himself experienced in separating his Son from himself for the ultimate good of the world he created. As he's done so many times before, God showed me again that he's been through my every heartache and made provision for my every need. That morning he gave me more than the encouragement I needed to get through my son's first day of kindergarten. He gave me deeper insight into the costly gift of his own Son on my behalf.

God knew that Jesus was eventually going to return home having completed his mission and having gathered many friends around him. It made me look forward to that evening when I'd be reunited with my own son. And it made me very, very grateful for the Best Bus Driver in the Universe—the One I knew I could trust to deliver him back to me safe and sound.

While we were helping Caleb through a major transition in his young life, God was helping us through a major transition in our own lives as parents. The God who doesn't change specializes in helping his children through change, and families who are connected to him develop the habit of managing life's transitions with trust and teamwork.

We all tend to paddle our own canoes a little more independently when the river of life is smooth. But the rapids and rocks of change remind us that there's a family expedition of canoes traveling together on the river and that if the canoes stay close and communicate, they can help each other survive until the water is smoother.

Life, of course, is a series of changes—starting kindergarten, going to summer camp, trying out for the basketball team, changing schools, going off to college, finding a job, starting a family, facing tragedies, dying. We know in advance that some of those changes are going to be simply wonderful. Others can't help but be difficult, even harsh. But nearly all of life's changes fall into the category of scary. And change is never scarier than when you feel you're facing it alone.

A devoted family navigates the changes of life together, and family members help one another through them. When one member is clinging to the doorknob of familiarity and security, another is there to assure him or her that it's OK to let go and venture out.

God shows us how this works. No matter what change we're facing, he basically says, "I've been there already, and I'm here to help you through it. Trust me."

> That is why we can say with confidence, "The Lord is my helper, so I will not be afraid. What can mere mortals do to me?"
>
> Remember your leaders, who first taught you the word of God. Think of all the good that has come from their lives, and trust the Lord as they do.
>
> Hebrews 13:6–8

God says that the best way to meet the scariness of change is with trust. And he says that godly leaders—like parents and mature family members—can be models. They not only demonstrate God's trustworthiness in their lives through changes of the past, but they can model trust in God as they meet future change.

> **A devoted family navigates the changes of life together, and family members help one another through them.**

In other words, devoted families help us make our sack lunches and fill our bags with school supplies. They walk us to the bus, and they are there waiting when it returns. Devoted families know the big changes of life are scary, but they've found a Bus Driver who is loving and capable, and they trust him to bring us home no matter how bumpy the ride.

Have you discovered the benefits of weathering change together as a family? Here are some things we've discovered that can make times like that most meaningful and effective.

Helping Your Family Practice Weathering Change Together as a Home Team

1. Lead Your Family to Anticipate and Prepare for as Many Major Life Changes as Possible

The wise look ahead to see what is coming, but fools deceive themselves.

Proverbs 14:8

Sometimes life's most regrettable decisions are made on the spur of the moment or out of passion or pressure. A life transition that could have been extremely positive—like choosing a college or a mate—can quickly turn negative or even disastrous because the preparation wasn't in place before the opportunity presented itself. The more you can help your family look ahead and prepare for times of significant change, the more smoothly and faithfully you are likely to navigate them.

While some of life's big transitions come unexpectedly, many others are somewhat predictable. Taking first jobs, going through puberty, driving, dating, going to college, moving out, getting married—these are examples of changes that families can often see coming and help one another prepare for in advance. Sure, there can be occasional surprises in the timing of these new chapters of life, but for the most part they needn't catch us or our families totally off guard.

In his insightful book *Raising a Modern-Day Knight*, author Robert Lewis writes about how Christian fathers can prepare their sons for Christian manhood. He makes the compelling point that many boys arrive at manhood without any real sense of what it means to be responsible, courageous, God-honoring leaders in their homes, churches, and world. Lewis maps out how a father can give his son things like a "vision for manhood," a "code of conduct," and a "transcendent cause" and then commemorate the son's growth from one stage of manhood to another with meaningful ceremonies.[2] That's a great example of the kind of steps a Christian family can take to prepare a child for the inevitable changes growing up will bring.

The Bible consistently urges us toward preparedness, whether it's storing up grain for the lean years, building a house on a rock, or being a wise steward who is ready for Christ's return. And there is great security in a family that is looking ahead, learning, planning, saving, and training for the future.

2. When Major Changes Come, Embrace the Opportunities to Be Used by God and to Trust Him

"Come over here," he said. So they came closer. And he said again, "I am Joseph, your brother whom you sold into Egypt. But don't be angry with yourselves that you did this to me, for God did it. He sent me here ahead of you to preserve your lives."

Genesis 45:4–5

While some people thrive on change, most of us resist its discomfort. But the Bible is full of people like Joseph who learned that change is often God's instrument of growth and opportunity. The key is often in forging ahead in faith, ready to give it your best shot and trust God for the outcome.

If you have had the pleasure of raising children into the later grades of school, you know the pressure of a big project that's due tomorrow. Often there are tears and regrets from the student and frustrated lectures from the parent and project rescuer. We've been through that experience a few times, and in the process I've learned at least one life principle. At some point we have to stop focusing on what we can't control and start focusing on what we can control.

That's often the lesson that devoted families have to urge upon those ready to parachute out into the scary skies of change. It's not the time to worry about flying the plane or changing the landing target. Focus on leaving the plane, count to ten, and pull the ripcord. The rest is flying and trusting God and the laws he's created.

I've often told my family about the time when my eighth-grade teacher lost her voice and drafted me to follow her around to all of her classes and be her mouthpiece. This sounds like a horrifying experience to them, a change that would be very difficult—going from student to teacher. But my family also now sees me speak and teach in front of large audiences, and I'm able to tell them that, truthfully, that day in eighth grade was a significant, though at first traumatic, time when I realized, *I can do this. I even kind of enjoy it. I'm told I'm good at it—and maybe God can use me this way.*

Encourage your family—and yourself—with examples from your past when significant change strengthened your character or placed you in a position to serve God in un-expected ways. And when they face their own potentially traumatic changes, help them open up their perspective and stretch toward the larger person God is helping them become.

3. Adapt

One day as Jesus was walking along the shore beside the Sea of Galilee, he saw two brothers—Simon, also called Peter, and Andrew—fishing with a net, for they were com-mercial fishermen. Jesus called out to them, "Come, be my disciples, and I will show you how to fish for people!" And they left their nets at once and went with him.

Matthew 4:18–22

When Jesus first called his disciples into the family of God, he asked them to make a significant life change. They left their homes, their professions, their security, and more. But Jesus promised them he would help them adapt to a new way of life, fishing for people.

When someone in your family faces significant change, he or she often needs help adjusting to live with the change. There can be an initial paralysis where the person facing the change simply says, "I can't do this." That's when a loving, devoted family who trusts in God can come alongside and with clearer vision show, and even do, some of the steps that will help navigate the change. When our son Caleb got to kindergarten that day, he could peel his own banana. He had adapted to meet the challenges of his new life at school.

> **There can be an initial paralysis where the person facing the change simply says, "I can't do this."**

This isn't just true of parents helping children. When my widowed grandma died several years ago, it was very difficult on my dad. It was all he could do to deal with her death and funeral, but then there were the tasks of sorting through her things, cleaning out and selling her house and car, and distributing and transporting items of value. I remember him sinking into her familiar recliner and saying, "I just don't know if I can do this." But I also remember his wife, his four children, and their families rallying around him, staying several days after the funeral, and helping him adapt in very practical ways to a new chapter of his life without his mom.

Families who are sensitive to the changes of life can help each other adapt in so many ways. I know loving spouses who have helped their mates shave their heads during cancer treatments. I know parents who have helped their children turn to music or another interest when they didn't make an athletic team. I know upperclassmen brothers who helped freshmen sisters manage the first week of high school. You probably do too. Chances are, if you can empathize with the change another family member is going through, you can help him or her adapt to it.

4. Add Unanticipated Perks to Unanticipated Change

> When doubts filled my mind,
>> your comfort gave me renewed hope and cheer.
>
> Psalm 94:19

There are times when our families can do very little to directly bear the load of change one member is bearing. We've prayed, empathized, and assisted with the change in the ways we know how, but the person simply needs to walk through the next steps alone. That's the time to provide indirect help through the encouragement of perhaps unrelated "perks." Make his or her favorite dessert. Take a break and go do something he or she loves doing. Give an unexpected gift.

As Mary Poppins once sang, "Just a spoonful of sugar helps the medicine go down." Not all change is like medicine. In fact, some change can be more like the spoonful of sugar. But many times, a change that's uncomfortable or unexpected can be softened by a perk that offers hope and cheer.

Many dentists understand this and now offer to clean your teeth with your choice of flavors. In fact, many orthodontists now offer fashionable choices of color and style for braces and retainers. We can learn from these professionals who specialize in healthy smiles.

Several years ago our family was planning to move to Georgia from Illinois, where my wife Beth had lived her entire life. We were assured of God's leading in the move, but it was difficult to put that much distance between us

143

and our family and friends. After running the numbers and counting the cost, I knew it was time to give my wife an elaborate gift to help communicate to her that I knew how big the change she was facing was. We decided to transfer some of the equity from our house in Illinois into a swimming pool at our new house in Georgia. It was one of the "someday" lifelong dreams Beth and I had shared even before we were married fifteen years earlier. During the days of stress, and even some doubt, as we were uprooting our lives in Illinois, we were able to look ahead and say to one another, "Yes, but there will be a pool there."

Psalm 94:19 says, "When doubts filled my mind, your comfort gave me renewed hope and cheer." In small and large ways, devoted families can provide comfort through perks or simply distractions that will encourage and make change more manageable.

5. Provide Oases of Security during Times of Significant Change

> David was staying in the stronghold at the time, and a Philistine detachment had occupied the town of Bethlehem. David remarked longingly to his men, "Oh, how I would love some of that good water from the well in Bethlehem, the one by the gate." So the Three broke through the Philistine lines, drew some water from the well, and brought it back to David. But he refused to drink it. Instead, he poured it out before the LORD.
>
> 2 Samuel 23:14–16

Few of us experience changes as dramatic as those David experienced. From shepherd boy to hero, from hero to king, from king to fugitive, from fugitive back to king—David lived through a lot of transition and uncertainty before handing a stable kingdom over to his son Solomon. The passage above tells us that during one of those stressful times, he simply longed out loud for something familiar, something that reminded him of a more peaceful, tranquil season of life. And those who loved him most went to great lengths to bring their king and friend that oasis. In their sacrificial act David found more comfort, encouragement, and security than even that for which he had longed could bring.

My wife recently told me that she has saved the tattered shirt Caleb wore that first day of kindergarten. When our son reads the story that opens this chapter, he'll be able to hold that shirt in his hands and remember a time when his family and his God stood by him during a significant time of childhood change. Perhaps it will be a little oasis of security for him as he faces the seemingly larger transitions ahead.

Does your family have oases of security to draw upon during times of transition? It may be a familiar place or a tradition you can return to. It may be people who aren't regularly in your life but have been a great support or encouragement to you in the past. Maybe you need to put your wife on a plane to visit her sister or insist that your husband call up his college roommate. Maybe you need to plan a family retreat to a place that will recall simpler, more secure times.

The interesting thing about David's oasis—the refreshing water his devoted men brought him—is that he didn't have to be in Bethlehem, and he didn't have to drink the water to have his longing satisfied. He had only to see that those closest to him heard his heart and were willing to do everything in their power to help him through a difficult time.

Earlier in this chapter I mentioned the change my dad had to embrace when his mother died. But my dad also told me about the change my grandma embraced on her deathbed. In the last few hours of her life with my dad at her side, she would raise up in her bed and with a delirious voice ask, "What are we going to do? What are we going to do? What are we going to do?" But then each time, my dad tells me, she would lie back on her pillow and answer her own question: "I guess we'll just trust the Lord."

Death is the biggest change life brings. In a sense, what my grandma faced on her deathbed is similar to what my son faced on our doorstep before he boarded the bus for kindergarten. The way my grandma faced that change teaches me a lot about how to help my family face all their smaller changes. Do all you can under the guidance of God's Word. And then just trust him.

Please *Do* Try This at Home

1. Make a list of future life changes for each member of your family—the changes you can anticipate. Then make preparing for those changes the topic of a series of family devotions. Have fun imagining family members at that future point in time and under those circumstances. And help them identify biblical principles that will help them prepare for and navigate those life transitions before they're upon them.

2. Identify members of your family who are going through significant times of change right now. What can you do to help them identify the opportunities for growth and service that can come from this change? What can you do to come alongside them and help them with the changes without robbing them of those growth opportunities? Choose teachable moments when life changes aren't breathing down their necks to point out the benefits of challenging times like

this. And then choose a way you can shoulder part of the burden of change with them.

3. Again, identify members of your family who are going through significant times of change right now. What perk could you give them to encourage them during this time? What oasis could you take them back to that would encourage them and bring back fond memories and feelings of security? Make plans to give them a perk or an oasis within the next few days.

9

Trading the Seat

The Practice of Fighting Together

A friend and I were talking once about families and fatherhood, and he mentioned that he had five children. "Wow, that sounds like a handful," I remarked, thinking about how busy our house was with our three boys. His response startled me a little.

"Actually," he said, "I've observed over the years that all families really have the same number of children."

"The same number? What do you mean?"

I could tell he was setting me up somehow, but I couldn't imagine how he could come up with that bizarre conclusion.

"No matter how many kids a family has, I've observed that it's always the same number: one too many."

I didn't know whether to laugh, scold him, or quietly slip away to call the Department of Children and Family

Services. What an unloving, or at least sarcastic, outlook for a father to have—especially a father with five children! Why on earth would this man with such a low view of children have five of them? And what must life be like for his wife and those poor kids?

My friend could tell from my concerned expression that my mind was running toward some pretty critical thoughts of him. So he decided he'd had enough fun and had better explain his unusual comment.

"Don't get me wrong," he smiled. "I love my kids—every one of them—and I'd do anything for them."

I was feeling a little reassured. He continued.

"But here's what happened with us. We had our first child, and he was wonderful. We couldn't believe the joy he brought into our life. And we even found it pretty easy to adjust to being parents and not just a couple. So we said, 'Hey, let's do this again!' And we had another child. Life got even better. Our older child loved the baby. We had already learned diapers and strollers and feeding and everything. Everything was great."

I was beginning to wonder if I was talking to someone with a multiple personality. This guy sounded like a great, loving father, not a dad who thought his kids were nuisances. I waited to hear more.

"So we decided to have three, and then four. Even with four children, we found life very manageable. Sure, we were busy, but somehow we seemed to have everything we needed to manage, and we managed pretty effortlessly. Our friends were amazed at how well we held things together. So we kept going. Number five was born."

"That's great," I interjected. "And so you guys are managing that busy household and enjoying it now?" I guess I had too quickly dismissed his initial remark.

"No, that's just it," he quickly replied. "Number five came along, and our life fell apart. It was like the proverbial straw that broke the camel's back. We had to buy a bigger car. In fact, we had to get an extra car so we could keep up with all the emerging schedules. We needed a bigger house. The oldest one's soccer schedule and the youngest one's feeding schedule pulled us in opposite directions. It was awful!"

As melodramatic as his description of life was, I could see that there was a faint smile and a twinkle in his eye as he spoke. He had been sort of pulling my leg—and describing a profound truth.

"You see," he continued, "every family really has the same number of children—one too many. The thing is, they don't know it's one too many until they have the last one. For some families that's five or eight or twelve." He paused for dramatic effect. "For some people, it's just one." He left that lingering thought out there long enough for me to picture a couple of families that seemed totally overwhelmed and consumed with their one child. Then he drove his point home.

> **Winning families find ways to work through conflict and to fight fair.**

"It's almost as if you're supposed to have a little more than you can handle in a family. When things are going smoothly, that's great. But when there's chaos or crisis or even conflict, that's when you have a chance to choose love. That's when you have a chance to stay engaged and work through things instead of escaping. That's when you really learn to hang together."

Though I had a little trouble accepting my friend's describing children like hot dogs—one too many will give you indigestion—the years since then have shown me over and over again the truth of the point he was making. Families have conflict. Siblings, in particular, are prone to it. And winning families find ways to work through conflict and to fight fair.

Our two oldest sons are only nineteen months apart, and they often illustrate for us intense love and companionship along with intense competition and rivalry. One day when Caleb was about four and Noah was about three, Noah decided for some reason that he wanted to sit in Caleb's car seat. Attempts to reason with him proved futile. He couldn't even express to us why he wanted the other seat so desperately. Finally Beth appealed to him with the simple truth: "But, Noah, that's your brother's car seat!"

Neither of us was ready for his mercenary retort: "Then I don't want him to be my brother!"

Beth looked at me as if to say that such extreme statements are to be handled by fathers. I cleared my throat to make room for the profundity that would emerge and then decided to use every dad's secret weapon—guilt.

"Why, Noah," I began with a serious tone, "are you saying you'd rather have Caleb's car seat than have him as a brother?"

Unfortunately, to Noah it may have sounded more like a legitimate offer than the rhetorical question I'd intended.

"Okay," he replied sweetly and proceeded to climb up into Caleb's car seat as if he expected me to go draw up the necessary papers to dismiss Caleb as his brother.

But if we were caught off guard by Noah's boyish declaration, we were even less ready for Caleb's response. He looked at Beth—probably feeling that I had not done the best possible job of negotiating his position in the matter—and said, "Mommy, I don't want to stop being Noah's brother. He can sit in my car seat."

That brief conflict and quick resolution has continued to be an example to me over the years of the amazingly petty things over which families can fight and the amazingly important practice of working through conflict in a way that values relationship over possessions or position.

What is causing the quarrels and fights among you? Isn't it the whole army of evil desires at war within you? You want what you don't have, so you scheme and kill to get it. You are jealous for what others have, and you can't possess it, so you fight and quarrel to take it away from them. And yet the reason you don't have what you want is that you don't ask God for it. And even when you do ask, you don't get it because your whole motive is wrong—you want only what will give you pleasure.

James 4:1–3

The Bible is pretty clear about what causes quarrels and fights among people, including families. It's the conflicting desires we have and the expectation that others are supposed to help us fulfill our desires.

From our basic sinful nature flows selfishness, and many times without even realizing it, we begin pursuing selfish desires through scheming and manipulating and fighting. When we don't get everything we want, we look around for someone to help us, and the first people in our line of sight are our family members. Sometimes we see that they have things we want, and then our desires are compounded with jealousy or envy.

> **The Bible is pretty clear about what causes quarrels and fights among people, including families.**

This is not a new problem. Sometimes we feel like our families can't be as perfect as we're sure those in the Bible are. But if you read the book of Genesis, for example, it's full of imperfect families who were plagued by selfishness and the deceit, manipulation, and conflict that flow from it. In fact, you read about more dysfunctional families in the Bible than you do about model families.

The Bible and human history in general demonstrate that families can really hurt one another and be driven apart if they don't learn how to handle these battling desires. Fortunately, James gives us not only an insightful analysis but also an inspired solution: We're supposed to ask God to meet our needs, and we're supposed to ask him with the right motive.

If we can learn to more consistently turn to God with our needs, and if we can make Christ-like character rather than our own comfort or pleasure our motive, it will take a lot of pressure off our families. But that's not what comes naturally. Selfishness is. So we need to help our families do things God's way. We need to take our desires to God and ask him to either fulfill them or change them.

Jacob was one of those imperfect family members in the book of Genesis who had to learn this the hard way. He wanted his father Isaac's blessing, the birthright blessing that was due to his older brother, Esau. Instead of going to God with his desire, he resorted to deceit and trickery to snatch it from his father and then had to run for his life to escape Esau's wrath (see Genesis 27–35 for the full story).

Although God's blessing was ultimately on Jacob's life, Jacob had taken things into his own hands and insisted on his own timing. He continued to live a life plagued by manipulation and trickery, and over the years his father-in-law and brothers-in-law began to resent him and feel cheated by him.

God then tells Jacob it's time to return home and that he will be with him as he goes. Jacob sets off for home with his family and possessions and sends an advance peace offering to his estranged brother. Esau responds by riding toward Jacob's camp with an army of four hundred men! Jacob is terrified but is caught between the broken relationships he's created on both sides of his family.

The night before the brothers reunite, Jacob wrestles with God beside the Jabbok River. He's still persistent, still aggressive, still desiring to be blessed by God. But this time he tells God about his desire instead of trying to manipulate what he wants from his family.

When Jacob comes to God with his desire, God begins to change his character. In fact, at that moment God changes his name from Jacob to Israel. Jacob then approaches his brother with humility and a penitent heart and finds forgiveness and restoration with Esau and peace for his family. There are many lessons for us in the life of Jacob.

Have you discovered the benefits of learning to manage conflict as a family? Here are some things we've discovered that can make times like that most meaningful and effective.

Helping Your Family Practice Managing Conflict Together as a Home Team

1. Train Your Family to Control Their Anger

And "don't sin by letting anger gain control over you." Don't let the sun go down while you are still angry, for anger gives a mighty foothold to the Devil.

Ephesians 4:26–27

A popular television comedy once featured an episode where two different families handled anger and conflict in two very different ways. One family yelled at each other and vented their anger whenever they had conflict. The other family suppressed their anger and pretended that offenses didn't really bother them. Throughout the episode the two families debated which approach is better.

Of course, neither of those approaches is healthy. Unrestrained anger is selfish and often does irreparable damage to others. Unexpressed anger builds up and eventually reveals itself in other hurtful ways.

This verse from Ephesians gives us a better way, the way we should coach our families. It assumes we will sometimes be angry but points out that anger becomes sin not when it merely exists but when it controls us. When Jesus threw the money changers out of the temple, he showed us that we can be angry without sinning. His anger was controlled and motivated by righteousness rather than selfishness. Others in the Bible, such as Moses, Samson, Samuel, and Jonathan, also show us a controlled, righteous anger. That's the way Ephesians 4:26–27 coaches us to deal with our anger. Control it and make sure it comes from righteous motives rather than selfish motives.

> **There are two important times to train our families about controlling anger: before it strikes and when it strikes.**

There are two important times to train our families about controlling anger: before it strikes and when it strikes. Before anger strikes we can help our families understand that it is a natural emotion, one that can be used for noble purposes. We can talk through what makes them angry and how they can recognize situations that create anger, and they can anticipate those situations so the anger doesn't take them by surprise and control them. Then when anger strikes it's important that we use our authority as parents to insist that anger be restrained from expressing itself in hurtful words or actions and that it is instead channeled in righteous expressions.

Ephesians 4:26–27 gives us a big help when it reminds us not to let the sun go down while we're still angry. Unresolved anger can fester into bitterness and resentment, and those are potentially more dangerous than the offense that caused the initial anger. If we are going to help our families manage the inevitable conflict that comes in family life, we must train them to recognize and control their anger.

2. Seek Understanding through Listening

Dear friends, be quick to listen, slow to speak, and slow to get angry. Your anger can never make things right in God's sight.

James 1:19–20

It's one thing to control anger when it strikes. It's quite another thing to do what James writes here and actually be "slow to get angry." How does that work? It seems to me there's a formula right in the verse. It looks something like this:

Quick to listen + slow to speak = slow to get angry

James seems to be saying that while anger is a natural reflex, we should work at making listening and restraint our supernatural reflex. When someone acts selfishly toward us, it's hard not to respond verbally right away. But this verse says that instead of retaliating with quick anger, or even quick words, we should be quick to listen.

Our goal in relationships should be to listen and understand so that when the people around us say or do offensive things, we don't have to flash our anger. Instead, we view their behavior in the context of what we know to be going on in their lives because we've been listening. The more in tune we are to the needs and perspectives of others in our families, the more tolerant we can be of their behavior.

Training our family members to listen and understand rather than respond with quick anger requires patience and consistency. When one family member does something selfish or offensive and another responds in anger, it's important to take the time right then and there to stop the fight and figure out what caused it. We must insist that everyone listen to one another until we can all figure out what happened and why it happened.

Over time, the more we learn to listen and understand before speaking, the more slowly we get angry. It takes time and practice, but consider what Proverbs says about the alternative: "Discipline your children while there is hope. If you don't, you will ruin their lives. Short-tempered people must pay their own penalty. If you rescue them once, you will have to do it again" (Prov. 19:18–19).

Short-tempered people—those who are quick to anger—tend to have problems their whole lives. Childhood is the time to teach our sons and daughters to listen to one another and search out the underlying sources of conflict rather than fighting on a purely emotional level.

3. Focus First on Words

We all make many mistakes, but those who control their tongues can also control themselves in every other way.

James 3:2

When I was a young boy, I had a treasure box. Actually, it was an old metal tackle box, and the things I kept in it were treasures only to me: my baseball cards, a pocketknife, a bag of rubber bands, a couple of neat rocks I had found, and a few special coins.

One summer morning I was rearranging my treasures, when my older brother, bored and looking for mischief, reached in and grabbed my little bag of rubber bands. He ran out the front door of our house with them in his hand, taunting me and making fun of my "stupid" treasures.

I followed him out the front door and onto our big front porch, but I had no hope of catching him. For that brief moment I forgot that we lived next door to the church where my dad was the pastor. I also forgot that there was a wedding at the church that morning. What I remembered was every word of profanity I had heard at school for the past several months, and finding no other weapons at hand, I yelled those words at the top of my lungs. I didn't know what they all meant, and they probably didn't make a lot of sense the way I used them, but there they were for every wedding guest on the front lawn of the church to hear coming from the pastor's front porch. The next thing I remember was my mother's hand slapped over my mouth as she dragged me on my heels back into the house.

Words are the currency in which mounting conflict is most easily measured. In healthy families the parents continually have their antennae out, monitoring the words that are tossed around, hopefully before they hit the front porch for everyone to hear.

Words are also the key to managing conflict in a family. Too often we treat words as a reasonable substitute for physical violence. But when we tolerate cruel, hurtful words—even those supposedly spoken in jest—we are really tolerating emotional violence. And while the scars words leave may not be as visible, they can be much deeper than we realize. That's why Paul wrote in his letter to the Ephesians,

> **Too often we treat words as a reasonable substitute for physical violence.**

> Don't use foul or abusive language. Let everything you say be good and helpful, so that your words will be an encouragement to those who hear them. . . . Get rid of all bitterness, rage, anger, harsh words, and slander, as well as all types of malicious behavior. Instead, be kind to each other, tenderhearted, forgiving one another, just as God through Christ has forgiven you.
>
> 4:29, 31–32

If we are to help our families manage conflict, we need to pay attention to the words our families use and bring them under control. It's up to us as parents to be vigilant about calling out unkind words or even sarcastic or disrespectful tones. Controlling our families' words is one preemptive key to keeping conflict manageable in our homes.

4. Model Self-Control over Your Own Words and Behaviors

A gentle answer turns away wrath, but harsh words stir up anger.

Proverbs 15:1

When it comes to relationships, these twelve words from Proverbs 15:1 are among the most intensely practical I've ever read. If our families would embrace and practice the truth of this one proverb, our ability to manage conflict together would greatly increase.

Over and over again I've seen conversations that were escalating to an angry crescendo suddenly diffuse into a reasonable, tender tone, all because someone dialed down the tone of his answer. He may still have been angry, or he may still have been on the right side of the argument. In fact, he may have been on the wrong side of the argument! But the mature composure to soften his answer made all the difference.

A gentle answer can have more power than the smartest argument or the cleverest witticism. It does more than reduce the sense of threat. It reminds everyone listening that emotion may be escalating but reason is a better path to resolution.

When parents demonstrate that kind of self-control in their own words and behaviors, they exert much more influence than if they merely entered the fray of anger and emotion. And when the rest of the family starts picking up on the power of a gentle answer, everyone will find family conflict much more manageable.

5. Know What's Worth Fighting For

Don't just pretend that you love others. Really love them.
Hate what is wrong. Stand on the side of the good. Love
each other with genuine affection, and take delight in hon-
oring each other. . . . Do your part to live in peace with
everyone, as much as possible.

Romans 12:9–10, 18

When families listen to one another, watch their words,
and control their anger, most conflict simply withers before
it can take root. Real fights are few and far between. But
even in that kind of winning family environment, there can
be occasional need for confrontation and even the loving
creation of conflict.

For example, what if a family member
starts getting involved in a problem relationship or self-destructive behavior he or
she doesn't see as dangerous? Or what if
a brother's wit starts crossing the line and
starts making jokes at a sister's expense?
Sometimes really loving someone means
confronting him or her and risking conflict for the sake of what is right.

> **Sometimes really loving someone means confronting him or her and risking conflict for the sake of what is right.**

Sometimes we avoid confrontation
and tell ourselves it's for the good of
the other person—that we wouldn't want to make him
uncomfortable or embarrass him. The reality is that we
usually avoid confrontation because it's uncomfortable for
us. And not confronting someone when he is engaging in a
dangerous or self-destructive behavior is an act of selfishness, not love or consideration.

Paul says that if we're going to really love people, we need
to hate what is wrong and stand on the side of good. That
kind of tough love means we speak up when a family member
is on the wrong path, even if that means some conflict.

161

No wonder Paul goes on to say that we should do our part to live in peace with everyone as much as possible. It's not that we're to stir up trouble or sit in judgment on others, especially our own family members. It's a matter of knowing what's not worth fighting over and what's very much worth fighting for.

There is one thing that is worth confronting, even fighting for, in a family, and that is each family member's personal relationship with God. In Luke 12 Jesus says that from that time forward, families would be divided over him. Some would accept him and follow him, and some wouldn't. Look at his surprising words: "Do you think I have come to bring peace to the earth? No, I have come to bring strife and division! From now on families will be split apart, three in favor of me, and two against—or the other way around" (vv. 51–52).

It's not that Jesus wants families to be divided. He came to reconcile us to God, and nothing helps us resolve our differences with each other more than first resolving our differences with God. But Jesus knows the sad reality that some family members will say yes to him and some will say no. And I think he's saying that the issue is important enough to risk family conflict rather than sweeping it under the rug.

In many families spiritual matters are informally or formally declared off limits because someone in the family just wants everyone to get along. But if someone in your family doesn't have a personal relationship with God through Jesus Christ, don't give up on that subject in the name of peace.

Please *Do* Try This at Home

1. For a day or two, focus on the words your family says to one another, and make note of any exchanges that seem potentially hurtful or less than loving. Make

a list of any word habits that seem to lead to conflict, even if they only seem like teasing at first. Decide if any of those words need to be declared off limits because of the hurt or anger they tend to generate.

2. The next time you find yourself in a conversation that is escalating in anger, consciously interject a gentle answer into the conversation. After things have cooled off, go back and show your family how a gentle answer can turn the tide in a heated conversation.

3. Make a list of family members who do not have a personal relationship with Jesus Christ. Is the subject open with them, or do they or other family members shut down discussions about spiritual things? Without seeking to be intentionally annoying or offensive to them, plan a gentle way to share your faith with them at the next opportunity, even if it risks some conflict. Be ready with plenty of gentle answers, but don't back down from your responsibility to share Christ with them.

10

Finding the Future

The Practice of Dreaming Together

Many young boys have a dream of playing big league baseball, and my friends and I were no different. The Newton Street baseball field where we honed our skills was a small-town classic. While its dirt infield got most of the action, left field had a gentle grass slope away from home plate that gave anything hit there home-run possibilities. And even though it was shorter, right field was a tantalizing target too, because across the street that formed its boundary was the chief of police's house. Anyone who chased a ball there was required to bring back plums from the tree in the yard, and that was about the most danger any of us had personally experienced at that stage in life.

The Newton Street baseball field was only a short bike ride from all our houses, and we spent many spring and summer days there, hitting, fielding, and dreaming. As much as we liked our little home field, we longed to be old enough to play Little League ball. Those games were played at the big, three-field American Legion Park out on the edge of town, where there were grass infields, dugouts, and even concession stands. We would look at our dusty blue jeans and tennis shoes and imagine the day when we'd be wearing matching uniforms, hats, and spikes. For our Newton Street gang, Little League was a necessary step on the road to the big leagues.

When the date for Little League tryouts finally rolled around, my mom drove me out to the big park at the edge of town and asked me what time she needed to pick me up. I proudly told her I wouldn't need a ride home that day. At the initial meeting the coach had said that he would take those who made the team down to the sporting goods store to get hats and lettering for the uniforms. We'd all be riding in the back of his big pickup truck. My best friend's dad managed the sporting goods store, and it was only two blocks from our house. No, I wouldn't need a ride home.

At the end of the tryout, the coach summoned everyone into the dugout. He thanked us all for coming out and said he was sorry everyone couldn't make the team that year. I looked around sympathetically at the handful of guys I thought probably wouldn't make it. Then the coach pulled a list out of his pocket, and one by one he called the names of the guys who made the team and asked them to run out to the pitcher's mound. Then he slowly folded the list and put it back in his pocket. He hadn't yet called my name.

It was one of those moments when you're sure there has been a dreadful mistake or a terrible miscarriage of justice, and it's all you can do not to shout out, "Wait! There's been a mistake! Check the list again . . ."

Behind the coach I could see two of my best friends, part of my Newton Street gang, high-fiving each other on the pitcher's mound. Then they looked back over to the dugout, and our eyes met. At first it was an excited, anticipating kind of look. Then, as they realized kids had stopped running out to the pitcher's mound, their expressions turned serious. They turned to each other in disbelief and then back to me. By that time tears were welling up in my eyes.

I'm sure the coach said some very comforting and reassuring words in those next few minutes, but I didn't hear any of them. My throat and eyes were burning, and it was all I could do not to start sobbing. Mercifully, the coach ended his little speech and dismissed us with an encouragement to try again next year. The other kids who were left in the dugout with me picked up their gloves and headed toward the parking lot. I picked up my glove too, anxious to escape the humiliation and disappointment. That's when I realized there wasn't a car waiting for me in the parking lot and there wouldn't be one. This was the fanciest ball field in town, but there were no phones there. I'm not sure I had ever felt more alone or more helpless.

I had felt the coach's eyes throughout this ordeal and knew he had noticed my shocked, then saddened, then helpless expression. He looked toward the parking lot and saw that I didn't have an escape vehicle. He then did the only thing he could do, and the worst thing he could do. He asked me if I needed a ride home. I looked out toward my friends and the elated team that I would not be playing with this summer, and I did the only thing I felt I could do. I lied and told him I didn't need a ride. Then started the long walk home.

Once I was out of sight, the sobbing came pretty uncontrollably. It took a mile or more for the tears to finally run out. Then there was just the disappointment and the growing realization that this summer was going to be awful. No uniform. No Little League. No friends. No baseball. I passed Newton Street on the way home, but I didn't stop.

When I arrived home, my mom and dad weren't entirely surprised at the disappointing outcome of the tryouts. I had told them that I had a little trouble hitting the fast pitching but that I was sure my fielding and speed on the base paths would earn me a spot on the team. Mom had wanted to meet me out at the ball field just in case, but she stayed home rather than communicating a lack of confidence in me.

> **The world is full of dream killers. But the family should be the biggest dream promoter and encourager there is.**

What amazed me was that the confidence she showed by staying home that day was not diminished one bit by the fact that I didn't make the Little League team. She and my dad mourned with me for a while about my disappointment, but before long they were talking about how athletic I was and how my sport was probably basketball rather than baseball. They began encouraging me to plant a new dream in my heart, and slowly a new can-do confidence returned the sparkle to my tearstained eyes.

That summer I began transforming my feeling of rejection over baseball into a new love for basketball. Later that love would bring me not only great enjoyment but honors, a college scholarship, and some of my life's best friendships. My family had helped me discover that Newton Street isn't the only place where dreams are created and that the Newton Street gang wasn't the only team that could help me follow my dreams.

The world is full of dream killers. But the family should be the biggest dream promoter and encourager there is. Our families should be like greenhouses for dreams, places where lots of possibilities can be explored and nurtured. When I tried out for the baseball team that day, I discovered that one of my seedlings wasn't quite strong enough to survive outside the greenhouse. But my parents gently replanted it (I made the baseball team the next year) and handed me another dream to keep my hopes alive.

Unfortunately, families can often be dream killers too. Even Jesus's family fell into that trap. Just as Jesus was beginning his public ministry, demonstrating his power and attracting a crowd, his family tried to bring him back to their version of reality:

> When Jesus returned to the house where he was staying, the crowds began to gather again, and soon he and his disciples couldn't even find time to eat. When his family heard what was happening, they tried to take him home with them. "He's out of his mind," they said.
>
> Mark 3:20–21

I'm sure that later, especially after Jesus's resurrection, his family was embarrassed by their lack of faith and confidence in him during those early days. And I'm sure their decision to try to take him home with them was made out of love and concern. They apparently thought he was deluded and didn't want him to humiliate himself or the family.

Sometimes the problem is that families are so familiar that we can't fully imagine the potential in our loved ones.

Sometimes the problem is that families are so familiar that we can't fully imagine the potential in our loved ones. We tend to confine them in the frame of reference we've seen them in for most of their lives, and when they're ready to step beyond that, it makes us uncomfortable. We have to remind ourselves that dreams can come true and that our loved ones' dreams deserve our support. We also may need to be ready for our loved ones to exceed our expectations or even our own achievements.

When we were first married, Beth taught third grade. She recently reminded me about a little girl in her class who was average to below average in many ways. But she tested exceptionally well in math. So Beth began to nurture and encourage her, and when parent-teacher conferences came along, she complimented the little girl's math aptitude to the mother. The girl's mother seemed a little surprised but grateful for the feedback. At the end of the school year, the mother sought Beth out and thanked her. "You really helped me recognize something exceptional in my daughter, something I'm not sure I would have noticed without your help. As I've encouraged her in math this year, she's really blossomed—and so has our relationship."

Teachers can be a great help to us parents in recognizing our children's gifts and dreams. And, of course, just listening to what our children get excited about and observing where their interests lie can give us additional insight. But sometimes children are quite unaware of or unable to articulate their dreams. It takes some keen observation from us parents, and maybe even a little detective work from time to time, for us to know how to help incubate the dreams our children are hatching.

Of course, children aren't the only family members with dreams. In fact, many times Mom or Dad may be sacrificing dreams or putting them on hold for the sake of the family. Maybe Mom wants to finish college, or Dad wants to start his own business. It's healthy for children to know their parents' dreams, and often they're more than ready to return the sacrifice to help Mom or Dad reach for the stars.

When the whole family knows each other's dreams, it can be surprising how much encouragement and teamwork starts to flow. Deep down we love each other and want each other to be happy and fulfilled. Sometimes we just need to find out what really matters to the ones we love so we know how we can help.

Have you discovered the benefits of dreaming together as a family? Here are some things we've discovered that can help.

Helping Your Family Practice Dreaming Together as a Home Team

1. Keep Affirming the Uniqueness of Each Family Member

For we are God's masterpiece. He has created us anew in Christ Jesus, so that we can do the good things he planned for us long ago.

Ephesians 2:10

Each member of your family is a masterpiece, hand-crafted by God for special purposes that were planned before he or she was born. We're all different, all unique, and that's a very positive part of God's plan.

In families it's sometimes more efficient or more convenient for everyone to be treated alike. And, of course, preferential treatment is something most parents know to avoid. But striving for fairness or equity among family members does not have to mean pressing for uniformity.

In our families we may have artists, athletes, musicians, entrepreneurs, and stand-up comedians. We may have introverts and extroverts, leaders and followers, people who think deeply and people who feel deeply, and, of course, combinations of all the above. Winning families affirm the uniqueness of each member and help them to be all they can be.

God knows each of us intimately, and he knows the unique way he put us together (see Ps. 139:15–17). But we don't have that complete knowledge of one another, so we have to mine it like gold in the context of an encouraging,

171

supportive relationship. And one of the most important mining techniques we have is to ask questions. With caring, insightful questions we can draw out the depths and dreams of another person. It takes time and trust, but it's very much worth the effort when we strike gold and uncover a significant nugget of who that God-crafted person is deep inside and what our role might be in encouraging his or her dreams and life purpose.

From the moment I first met Beth on our college campus, I wanted to get to know her better. Unfortunately, I quickly discovered that she had a boyfriend back home. Still, she gave me a glimmer of hope. We couldn't date, she said, but we could still get to know each other better. I remember thinking that she was just being nice, and I pretty much gave up on the idea that our relationship would be able to go much further.

> **Take time to ask questions that "mine the gold" in the people you care about.**

Then came that Friday afternoon when everything changed. Beth was coming out of the cafeteria with her friends. I was going into the cafeteria by myself. We paused just outside the door to exchange hellos, then walked our separate ways to the sound of her friends' giggling. I remember shaking my head again with fresh disappointment that our relationship had been drenched before it could be kindled.

Moments later I turned around in the cafeteria line and saw her approaching, this time by herself. She asked if she could join me, and for the next half hour she got to sit and watch me eat spaghetti. Then we walked outside and sat down on a fairly remote bench. Somehow, I felt the future of our relationship was on the line, and I wondered what I could possibly say to keep it alive.

Because Beth eventually became my wife, I tend to believe that the question that came to my mind during that nervous moment was providentially inspired. As we sat down and looked at each other with that "now what?" look, I simply asked her to tell me about her favorite things.

For the next four hours, we exchanged favorite things. She talked about rainbows, her puppy, sunsets, evening walks, and her love-worn teddy bear. I talked about basketball, writing, music, and making people laugh. A few weeks later I sang her a song I had written about her favorite things. Within a month the boyfriend back home was history.

Take time to ask questions that "mine the gold" in the people you care about. Look for the uniqueness in each person. Try to discover what ignites his or her passion and what dreams God may have buried inside. You won't be disappointed in the result.

2. Help Each Family Member Envision and Discover God's Purpose for His or Her Life

"For I know the plans I have for you," says the LORD. "They are plans for good and not for disaster, to give you a future and a hope."

Jeremiah 29:11

The more we understand the unique way God has crafted each member of our families, the more we'll begin seeing the purposes he may have planned for their lives. Have you ever played the party game where you're handed a mysterious object and asked to figure out what it is and what it's used for? You know it's special. You know it's been handcrafted and that no one would create one of those by accident. But out of context it's really hard to describe the particular use or purpose of that object. That can be what it feels like to look at your children sometimes. How on earth will you help them discover what they were made for, what God's purpose is for their lives?

There are a number of ways the purpose of that party-game object could be discovered. Hopefully, someone in the group has experience with that object and has seen it in its context. If so, they may simply declare, "I've seen one of those before—here's how it's used." Or, if no one has direct experience with the object, the group members can use their collective intelligence to speculate on its use. If the object has a household use, they can even get up and compare it to a similar object that's already in use.

If no one has a clue what it is or where to look for a similar item, they may just have to give up as far as the game is concerned. But if they were committed to discovering that object's purpose, they could research it and compare it to other objects and ask questions at the hardware store or the FBI or the Library of Congress—and eventually they would find someone who knew the purpose for which the object had been designed.

We may have to do all of that and more with our families. Few things in life are more worthwhile than helping those we love discover the purpose for which God created them.

To quote again from Rick Warren's *The Purpose-Driven Life*, "God never does anything accidentally, and he never makes mistakes. He has a reason for everything he creates. Every plant and every animal was planned by God, and every person was designed with a purpose in mind."[3] I enthusiastically recommend this book to anyone seeking to discover his or her life purpose and to parents desiring to help their families with that process.

3. Fan the Flames of Your Family's Dreams with Encouragement

I know that you sincerely trust the Lord, for you have the faith of your mother, Eunice, and your grandmother, Lois.

This is why I remind you to fan into flames the spiritual gift God gave you when I laid my hands on you. For God has not given us a spirit of fear and timidity, but of power, love, and self-discipline.

2 Timothy 1:5–6

Affirming the uniqueness of each family member and helping him or her discover his or her life purposes are not overnight tasks. In fact, they are really tasks that have to be measured over a lifetime. But there is a task that can be measured on a daily basis—the task of encouragement.

Remember that often the family members whose dreams we are trying to encourage don't have a clear idea of what they want themselves. They have little sparks of interest here and there but don't know what to do with them or even how long they'll last. Our responsibility and joy as parents is to fan the sparks we notice. Then if our fanning produces a small flame, we add encouragement like kindling and the resources they need to succeed like fuel. One day, when we stand in the full heat and warmth of their fulfilled dreams, we'll remember with satisfaction the words of encouragement that first fanned that spark into a flame.

I was once visiting a college friend and getting reacquainted with his son Nick while dinner was being prepared. As we talked, Nick's younger sister Gail walked in.

"Hey, squirt!" Nick punctuated his greeting with a good-natured poke at her side.

"Stop it, you," Gail protested, but the smile behind her pout made it clear that she enjoyed her older brother's attention.

"Hey, Gail, I haven't seen you since you got out of the hospital—how's it going?" I asked.

My question wasn't meant to embarrass her, but the way she ducked her head and mumbled a quick "OK" let me know she didn't want to say more about it. But Nick did.

"Oh yeah, she's doing great now. She ought to be after all the time they spent fixing her up in the hospital and all the money it cost to do it."

Nick's report on his sister's series of treatments and operations was intended to be an honest, fact-filled answer to my question. He went on to tell me the details of her rare disease, the process of discovering and diagnosing it, and the trauma the whole family had been through when it almost took Gail's life.

Nick also seemed really preoccupied with how much his sister's treatment and hospitalization had cost. "Dad figures the total is close to twenty thousand dollars!" Nick exclaimed. "I mean, just think of what we could do with that much money!"

Nick did not notice the effect his medical and financial report was having on his sister. Gail's pale complexion was hardly visible anymore as she buried her face in her hands. Her frail frame looked even smaller as she slumped farther into her chair.

I knew Nick wasn't intending to hurt his sister. In fact, it was easy to see how much he loved her and had feared losing her during her illness. If Nick had stopped to think, he would have realized that he was unwittingly implying that the money involved was huge and awesome and that his sister was small and inconsequential by comparison.

"So you're saying this little girl cost your family twenty thousand dollars?" I said, giving Nick a chance to be quiet and listen to what his words implied.

"Uh, well, sort of . . ." Nick's hedging reply showed he would have loved to have some of those words back.

"But worth every penny, right?" My question made Gail's face lift quickly, and her eyes darted to Nick, waiting for his reply.

"Well, of course. Worth every penny and a whole lot more!" Nick exclaimed.

I wish you could have seen the look on Gail's face. It was worth about twenty thousand dollars—maybe more. And Nick's grateful glance let me know that he realized he needed to fan his sister's flame rather than extinguish it.

Recently I was at a retreat where the leader asked us to participate in a very interesting group exercise. Half of us were placed in a circle of chairs, with the other half standing outside the circle. The leader then asked those who were standing to think of something they wished they had heard more often from the people who were important to them while they were growing up. Then he asked them to whisper that something in the ear of the person sitting in front of them. After doing that, they were to rotate one person to the right until they had whispered those words in the ear of everyone seated in the circle.

> **Our families need to hear our words of encouragement. And they need to hear them often. More than we realize, their dreams depend on it.**

As I sat with my eyes closed in the circle, I was amazed and moved at what I began to hear in whispered tones. So many people wished that their fathers had said they loved them. Others felt condemnation or criticism because their parents rarely complimented them. Many said they lacked confidence because a parent had rarely said something as simple as "Good job, honey."

Our families need to hear our words of encouragement. And they need to hear them often. More than we realize, their dreams depend on it.

4. Steer Your Family Away from Materialism

Don't store up treasures here on earth, where they can be eaten by moths and get rusty, and where thieves break in and steal. . . . Wherever your treasure is, there your heart and thoughts will also be.

Your eye is a lamp for your body. A pure eye lets sunshine into your soul. But an evil eye shuts out the light and plunges you into darkness. If the light you think you have is really darkness, how deep that darkness will be!

Matthew 6:19, 21–23

This may seem like an unusual point to mention in the context of helping your family dream together. But I believe materialism can be a major barrier to the dreams God has placed within our families' hearts. They may need our encouragement and permission not to submit their dreams to the constraints of material rewards.

Jesus had a lot to say about money, and in this passage from the Sermon on the Mount, he clearly says money can be the chief rival of God in choosing the course of our lives and our dreams. It can cloud our vision and keep us from seeing God's perfect plans for us. And many times we don't even realize it.

Think about it—does God really have the freedom to lead us and our families anywhere he might choose? Or do we have certain parameters of comfort or annual income in which God's leadership must fit? What if our sons' or daughters' dream, and God's purpose for them, was to take the gospel to a people who had never heard it before? What if that straight-A student is designed by God to be a doctor in Haiti rather than in the American suburbs? What if that gifted teacher wants to teach inner-city children and takes our grandchildren to live down in that part of the city with them?

Many times, out of genuine love and concern for our families, we unwittingly prioritize their comfort over their character. As we help our families dream together, we don't want to put any limitations on where God may lead them. And that may mean rethinking our own values as well as steering our children.

5. Equip Your Family to Keep Following Their Dreams When You're Not Around

> But this is the new covenant I will make
>> with the people of Israel on that day, says the Lord:
> I will put my laws in their minds
>> so they will understand them,
> and I will write them on their hearts
>> so they will obey them.
> I will be their God,
>> and they will be my people.
> And they will not need to teach their neighbors,
>> nor will they need to teach their family,
>> saying, "You should know the Lord."
> For everyone, from the least to the greatest,
>> will already know me.
>
> Hebrews 8:10–11

There are so many things we need to give our children before they leave home and before we as their parents leave this life. They need faith, wisdom, values, hope, biblical training, relationship skills—the list goes on and on. No wonder parents never really feel like the job is done when the time comes for children to leave home. If those children are to continue following their dreams, we must strive to make sure they develop an essential gift at home and take it with them into life—the gift of confidence.

If confidence is like water, then kids are like sponges. No matter how much we try to pour into their lives, they can always soak up more.

If confidence is like water, then kids are like sponges. No matter how much we try to pour into their lives, they can always soak up more. Maybe that's because the pressure and circumstances of life so easily squeeze confidence out of us. Our children can be saturated when they leave for school in the morning and squeezed dry when they come home.

Given that rate of consumption, how can we ever let go of our children? Where would they ever find enough confidence to go more than a day or two without us? The answer, of course, is that each year they live with us, they have to gradually dig their own wells and tap into their own water supplies. While parents are wonderful sources of confidence, "portable" confidence must ultimately come from God.

In Hebrews we read about the qualities of the new covenant God has made with his people. It's a covenant that can be internalized and personally owned. It's a covenant that doesn't require priests or go-betweens.

That description of how God works these days encourages me by reminding me that he goes with my children not only after they leave my home but after I leave their world. I may have contributed a lot to their sponges, but I know where the refreshing water of confidence came from, and if I've shown them how to fill their own sponges, I know they'll have the confidence they need to follow their dreams, even when they are beyond my reach.

My wife and I have good friends who are the parents of two wonderful daughters. Our lives intertwined as their daughters babysat for our boys, and we watched with interest as the older daughter, Meredith, finished high school and headed off to college and then graduate school. Meredith is very intelligent, but she also seemed soft-spoken and shy in groups, and we wondered how this sweet young lady would fare away from her parents and so far from home.

Recently I asked Meredith's dad how she was doing, and he said she was doing great. A faint smile crossed his face, and I asked him what he was thinking about.

"Meredith's coming home next week on break," he said.

"Oh, good!" I replied. "We'd love to see her."

"I don't think she'll have time," he continued, and he then paused as if waiting to deliver a punch line. "She and her sister, Rachel, are camping out downtown so she can audition for *American Idol*."

I'm sure my jaw dropped several inches as I tried to picture sweet, demure Meredith in a flashy costume, strutting across a stage and crooning out lyrics that would not be found in their church's hymnal.

Meredith's dad enjoyed my surprise, and I got the idea he was a little surprised too. Meredith didn't intend to go to Hollywood—that wasn't her dream. She was in graduate school, studying journalism, and had concluded that this was a once-in-a-lifetime experience she could both write about and tell her grandkids about one day.

What encouraged me about Meredith's audition—and I'm sure it encouraged her dad even more—was that it demonstrated a great return on the investment of confidence her family had placed in her life. Her younger sister, Rachel, was going along to help her with her hair and makeup and costume—and perhaps to pick up a little extra confidence along the way.

I shook my head and smiled. "She's come a long way, hasn't she?" I said. With fatherly pride and gratitude, my friend agreed.

If Meredith could audition for *American Idol*, who knows what my children will be able to do by the time they leave home? The thought of it made me smile.

Please *Do* Try This at Home

1. At dinner some night this week, lead your family in an exercise of affirming one another's uniqueness. Choose a family member to start with, and ask everyone around the table to name one positive attribute of that person. They can include gifts, skills, character

traits, interests—anything that is special about that person. No doubt some jokes will flow, but don't let anyone turn the exercise negative, and don't let the person being described tear himself or herself down or refuse the affirmation being expressed. After going around the table two or three times, move on to the next person. Make sure to close with your own sincere words about how unique and special each member of your family is.

2. During family devotions or mealtime, or while you're traveling together as a family, tell the story of how you chose your profession or job and what you learned in the process. In addition, tell your family one or two dreams you haven't yet realized but would like to. Using your own example, help your family see how the life process of following your dreams works.

3. Identify something your children normally do with your help but that they're ready to do on their own. Maybe it's brushing their teeth or preparing a meal or staying home alone longer than normal. Choose something age appropriate that you can encourage them to do, and after they're successful, affirm their growing independence and confidence.

11

Ringing the Bell

The Practice of Serving Together

You don't have to know a lot about human nature to know that taking and consuming come naturally and giving and serving are learned behaviors. Among the hallmarks of immaturity are selfishness and immediate gratification, and families in which these are allowed to prevail are often unhappy and dysfunctional.

Since the time our children were old enough to walk, Beth has been actively engaged in teaching them to practice charitable habits. Because her primary spiritual gift is giving, she has a sort of supernatural intuition about what people need. So for years now she has guided us in family ministry projects that are fun, age appropriate for our kids, and genuinely helpful to others.

Sometimes those projects lead me outside my comfort zone, like the time she told me she had signed up our family to ring the bell for the Salvation Army at Christmastime. Our assigned station was in the center of the largest shopping mall in town, where Beth felt our two older sons would find a safe, warm place to learn service and hopefully see generous giving in action.

Beth made it clear that I did not have to participate in this activity, but I felt a little nervous about sending them out alone. I also reasoned that they would no doubt need my know-how to help raise a decent amount of money. They'd need coaching on where to position the pot, how to make eye contact and smile, how to answer questions that might arise, and so forth.

Boy, was I wrong. All those two little boys needed were Santa hats on their heads and bells in their hands. Cuteness and the Christmas spirit took over from there, and we watched in amazement as some of the most hurried and grumpy Christmas shoppers you can imagine stopped, laid down their packages, and dug deep to respond to the pleading eyes of those two little guys. Many, many people not only gave but also stopped long enough to place their donation in the hand of one of our sons and let him drop the money in the pot. They were clearly responding on a personal level to the boys and their act of service and not just to the charitable cause. In fact, as time passed, Beth and I learned that the more we just stood back from the boys and let them ring the bell and talk to people, the more people seemed willing to stop and give.

The Thanksgiving and Christmas holidays are especially wonderful times to participate in hands-on service and giving, and many times churches will provide family-friendly opportunities. We've been delighted to see how readily our kids rise to these occasions, whether it's filling shoe boxes with gifts for children overseas, buying Christmas gifts for the children of those in prison, or donating food for delivery to needy families. As we've personalized these activities together, we've also discovered the joy of doing these things as a home team.

But no experience of serving together has blessed us more than the experience of helping a new church get started. While our sponsoring church was somewhat traditional, it had a desire to reach the unchurched in a nearby community. Our family was one of four families that began meeting and praying together to discern what kind of church would be most inviting to those who didn't know God personally or had dropped out of church for some reason.

The yearlong process of praying and planning and preparing was very much a family experience. Among our four families we had babies, toddlers, children, teenagers, and young adults. We took turns meeting in homes to do our planning and work, and the older children helped with the younger children while the adults met.

About six months into our planning, we launched three neighborhood Bible studies that grew our core group to about forty people. That brought us grandparents, singles, parents, and teens of all ages. Then a year after our four families started meeting, we held our first public service in a local grade school. Through publicity and personal invitations, we invited people to a come-as-you-are, informal setting. There they found contemporary music, a creative children's program, and practical Bible teaching. That first Sunday 182 people came to church. By the end of the first year, almost 600 people had attended at least once. Our sponsoring church, whose attendance was about 120 at that time, rejoiced over the return on their investment in us.

In the two years we were involved in that church start, dozens of people entered a relationship with God through Jesus Christ. We baptized people in swimming pools and had Bible studies in school hallways. We saw people who hadn't been to church in over twenty years commit their lives to Christ and become active in discipleship and Christian service. It was the most challenging and spiritually rewarding time of my life.

I write about it here to describe the effect it had on our family as we served together. I can still picture our seven-year-old and our five-year-old helping set up chairs in the gym where we met. We had no storage space in the school, so every week we had to carry in our sound system and supplies, and I remember our two-year-old dutifully pushing a big plastic tub down the hall to a children's class. Each week my behind-the-scenes wife, who is so much better at remembering names and dates than I am, would stand by my side at the welcome table and whisper the names of approaching people in my ear so I could greet them more personally.

After the worship service it took a long time to dismantle the "portable church" we had set up, and lunch was usually pretty late on Sundays. But everyone in our family—and in many other families—pulled together and did church the hard way so that people in our community could have a chance to hear the gospel in a way and in a place that was accessible to them.

So many of the practices described in this book—eating together, working together, changing together, hurting together—happened every week in our family's life because we had found this unique, wonderful place of service. This local church gave us an "extended family"—a larger home team, really—where we practiced the same disciplines of growing together. In many ways, a local church is just a larger Christian family—one with even more opportunities to serve and mature together. What happened in the lives of the families we were reaching was wonderful, and in some ways miraculous. What happened in our family's life as we served together was wonderful and miraculous too. We grew closer and matured spiritually because we served together on Christ's own "home team"—his church.

We all want to have great families. But we may mean different things when we say "great." Recently I needed to do some research on the concept of greatness for a talk I was preparing. I decided to look at what the Bible, and specifically Jesus, said about greatness. It didn't take nearly as long as I thought it would. If you scour Jesus's words, you will find two criteria for greatness.

The first one is obedience. Jesus says,

> So if you break the smallest commandment and teach others to do the same, you will be the least in the Kingdom of Heaven. But anyone who obeys God's laws and teaches them will be great in the Kingdom of Heaven.
>
> Matthew 5:19

The second is service:

> But Jesus called them together and said, "You know that in this world kings are tyrants, and officials lord it over the people beneath them. But among you it should be quite different. Whoever wants to be a leader among you must be your servant, and whoever wants to be first must become your slave. For even I, the Son of Man, came here not to be served but to serve others, and to give my life as a ransom for many."
>
> Matthew 20:25–28

When we go to God for his definition of greatness, our own definition gets turned upside down. It's not about ambition and accomplishment; it's about humble obedience and service. That's the key to having a great family as well.

Not only does God's definition of greatness turn ours upside down, but his demonstration of grace toward us turns our lives inside out. It's not about us. It's about God and serving the people for whom he died. We don't have to be selfish anymore.

When we start looking for meaningful ways to turn our lives inside out, we realize that we need to find some pathways to service. That's one of the reasons God gave us our local churches—to give us opportunities and cooperation with other families who are seeking to serve. You see, a good church will have a meaningful worship service and an enjoyable and challenging pastor. It will take good care of our kids and provide us with encouraging Christian friends. There are many benefits to being part of a good church. But a *great* church will help us give our lives away.

Families partnering together in a great church that is committed to giving itself away discover that they can have a ripple effect on their entire world, and for all of eternity! Jesus said it this way in Acts 1:8, his last words on earth before he ascended into heaven: "But when the Holy Spirit has come upon you, you will receive power and will tell people about me everywhere—in Jerusalem, throughout Judea, in Samaria, and to the ends of the earth."

When we start looking at the world and our purpose in it that way, our entire perspective on our lives' mission and purpose is transformed. In fact, our lives never have more meaning and significance than when we join God in his worldwide, history-long purpose.

Have you discovered the benefits of serving and being on mission together as a family? Here are some things that we've discovered can help.

Helping Your Family Practice Serving and Being on Mission Together as a Home Team

1. Show Your Children the Character Qualities of a Servant

Don't be selfish; don't live to make a good impression on others. Be humble, thinking of others as better than yourself.

Don't think only about your own affairs, but be interested in others, too, and what they are doing.

Your attitude should be the same that Christ Jesus had. Though he was God, he did not demand and cling to his rights as God. He made himself nothing; he took the humble position of a slave and appeared in human form. And in human form he obediently humbled himself even further by dying a criminal's death on a cross.

Philippians 2:3–8

If our families are going to be drawn to acts of service together, they must see in us, and in other Christian leaders in their lives, the character qualities Jesus demonstrated when he took on the form of a servant. They must see the primary character quality of love demonstrating itself in the character qualities of humility and sacrifice. Ask yourself, Who do I know who consistently demonstrates the humility of Christ in service, and how can I put my family in a position to learn from that person?

> **Ask yourself, Who do I know who consistently demonstrates the humility of Christ in service, and how can I put my family in a position to learn from that person?**

Many times the heroes we adopt in our families are not those who demonstrate humility and selflessness. And in many popular arenas of life—sports, entertainment, politics, science, academics—there are plenty of self-serving examples. But I have also been encouraged to find that in these same arenas of life where ambition and pride tend to dominate the characters of the rich and famous, there are usually at least a few heroes who choose the opposite. In our family we try to seek out those heroes. We cheer hard for them, and we look to their example.

Winning families should also make sure to point with respect and admiration to the pastors, Sunday school teachers, and school and civic leaders who demonstrate Christ-like character. We need to let our families see us listening to them, reading their words, and following their example. If we don't actively and visibly respect and cooperate with leaders who model Christ-like character, our families are not likely to do so either.

Most importantly, though, our families must see Christ-like love, humility, and sacrifice in our own characters. As Jesus said in Matthew 20, the "natural" way for those in authority to act is to lord it over those in their charge. Do we lord it over our families, or do we humbly serve them? James 4:10 says, "When you bow down before the Lord and admit your dependence on him, he will lift you up and give you honor." That is the way to lead our families, with honor that comes from humility before God and others.

2. Train Your Family to Serve, Especially through Your Church

> So don't get tired of doing what is good. Don't get discouraged and give up, for we will reap a harvest of blessing at the appropriate time. Whenever we have the opportunity, we should do good to everyone, especially to our Christian brothers and sisters.
>
> Galatians 6:9–10

I will never be able to read these verses from Galatians 6 without thinking of my grandfather. This was perhaps his favorite passage of Scripture, and I can remember him quoting it my whole life. Granddaddy was a servant leader not only as a superintendent of schools but also as a deacon and teacher in his church, as a father and grandfather to his children, and as a husband to his wife. He was a man of strong and humble character. It really was his life ambition to never tire of doing what is good and to never give up a life of service.

At the dinner table Granddaddy was always serving, always hosting. "Won't you have some more meat? Did you get enough beans? How about some more bread?" I found myself wanting to return to my grandparents' home as often as possible, even after I lived eight hours away and had children of my own. I guess I didn't actually believe that sitting on my grandparents' laps would help my kids catch their character, but I know I believed that allowing my kids to know them even a little would help me train my family in the practice of serving others.

During one of those precious visits when just our family was there, the doorbell rang as we sat visiting in the living room. It was Denny, a man in his midseventies who introduced himself as their deacon from church. At first I thought how inconvenient it was that someone would drop in during our short family visit, but my grandparents seemed delighted to see him and to introduce us. He came in and stayed awhile.

During the twenty minutes or so Denny was there, the conversation was pretty routine—the weather, farm prices, ailments of people they knew. After a pleasant visit Denny leaned forward in his chair and said he needed to be going. He just wanted to look in on my grandparents and make sure they were doing okay and had what they needed. Before he stood, though, my granddaddy asked Denny if he would lead us in prayer. Granddaddy never did good-nights or good-byes without taking time for a devotional moment.

Denny kind of ducked his head and said, "Aw, Mr. Hooks, you know how I get." I had no idea what he meant, but my granddaddy (a.k.a. Mr. Hooks) must have, because he replied that he knew what Denny meant but it would mean a lot to him if he would pray for them before he left. Reluctantly Denny agreed, and as I started to bow my head I saw him reach into his back pocket and quietly pull out a huge red bandanna. It was the kind you see more often in the western Kentucky small town where my grand-parents lived than in the suburban neighborhood where my family lived, the kind that a farmer wraps around his head on a hot summer day or ties around his finger when his work draws some blood. Faded and worn at the edges, this red bandanna clearly had been used faithfully for a long time.

Denny's prayer was short and direct, a few words of rev-erence and adoration for his heavenly Father and a simple request that God's grace would continue to minister to my grandparents' household. The prayer took a few minutes, though. Denny cried through every word of it. That's why he needed the red bandanna.

Afterward, Denny left quietly with a warm smile and handshake for each of us, but he gave no explanation for his outpouring of emotion. It had clearly been a moving experience for my grandparents as well. After a few minutes of what felt like hallowed silence, they explained that ever since a significant event in Denny's life, he hadn't been able to come to God in prayer without weeping. He had asked to be excused from public prayers at church because he felt his emotion would be a distraction to others.

Those twenty minutes were the only time I've ever spent with Denny, but from the moment he walked slowly out my grandparents' door, I knew I wanted to be like him. On a hot summer afternoon when most seventy-year-olds would have been home in a recliner, he had been out serving and bringing comfort and blessing to two elderly saints who couldn't get out to church anymore. And he had given me a standard by which to measure my service to others. And I was very grateful that my family got to see his example.

Today a red bandanna I bought after meeting Denny in my grandparents' home rests on the Bible I use for my quiet time. It represents the kind of humble church service and fervent prayer to which I aspire. And it represents to me the responsibility we all have as parents to train our children in service through the church and to lead them in serving together as a family.

3. Serve with the Right Motives

Take care! Don't do your good deeds publicly, to be admired, because then you will lose the reward from your Father in heaven.

Matthew 6:1

Unfortunately, there can be wrong reasons for serving. In Matthew 6 Jesus says we should be careful to avoid good deeds that come from selfish motives. But he goes on to tell us how we can check ourselves to make sure our motives are pure: "But when you give to someone, don't tell your left hand what your right hand is doing. Give your gifts in secret, and your Father, who knows all secrets, will reward you" (vv. 3–4).

Jesus says the safeguard against improperly motivated service is to serve and give quietly, even secretly. This is an important principle to teach your family. Financial giving should be generous but private. Service should be sacrificial, not boastful.

It may seem like guiding our families in this way is difficult if we try not to call attention to our own service. One solution is to direct our families' attention to others we know who are quietly serving or giving in this way. But it's also true that our families will notice our attitudes and actions of service even if they don't see all the details. They'll know when we are at church for service responsibilities. They'll know how we respond when a need arises that calls for some special sacrifice. They'll see the way we're willing to serve humbly at home.

Secret service can infiltrate every day of our lives if we want it to. We can pack two towels in our gym bag in case someone forgets his. We can clean up extra trash at the fast-food restaurant, not just our own. We can give to good causes when they come our way, rather than resenting those who ask.

I remember one winter evening when I walked out into our office's parking lot and was startled by all the snow. I had worked later than usual that night and had been so busy I hadn't really noticed the steady, heavy blanket of white that had been accumulating.

Secret service can infiltrate every day of our lives if we want it to.

I had a little trouble even finding my car, though there were only a handful of others left in the parking lot. They all looked alike: huge white marshmallows on wheels, with no color or identifiable characteristics evident to distinguish one from another.

Remembering approximately where I had parked, I walked toward the marshmallow that most closely resembled my little car's size and shape. A swipe of my glove revealed that I had made the right choice, and a couple of minutes later I had started the engine and climbed back outside with my brush and window scraper. The soft, fluffy coating came off so easily that I was almost disappointed when I finished so quickly. Then I looked around at the three other cars left in the parking lot.

One of the cars belonged to my friend Julie. I had just said good-bye to her, and it looked like she was going to be there working for quite a while yet. I remember thinking that she had endured an even harder day than I had, and hers still wasn't over.

Clearing off her car was great fun. I guess it was because I could picture her coming outside, being shocked like me at the amount of snow, perhaps worrying about trudging around in a dark, vacant parking lot—and then seeing her car all cleared off and ready to go. Imagining her smile made me smile too. Cleaning off the other two cars was also fun, though I didn't really think about why at the time.

A day or two after I cleared off her car, Julie figured out who must have done it and asked me about it. It was gratifying to hear her words of appreciation and see in her eyes the type of admiration usually reserved for selfless acts. But Jesus's words tell me that perhaps my act of clearing off the other two cars had an even greater value—one I won't fully know until the day he rewards me for the good things I choose to do when nobody else is watching.

4. Train Your Family to Share Their Faith as They Serve

You are the light of the world—like a city on a mountain, glowing in the night for all to see. Don't hide your light under a basket! Instead, put it on a stand and let it shine for all. In the same way, let your good deeds shine out for all to see, so that everyone will praise your heavenly Father.

Matthew 5:14–16

Service for service's sake has value. Service for the sake of sharing the gospel message and pointing people to God has great eternal value. As we lead our families to serve together, we should also look for ways those acts of service can become bridges over which the good news about Jesus can travel.

Jesus says that our acts of service are to be humble and quiet, not proud or conceited. But he also says that in our service to others we carry a message that must not be hidden. It's the message of why we serve—that Jesus has made a miraculous difference in our lives and turned our definition of greatness upside down and our motivations inside out. Our good deeds are to take the attention they attract and

> Service for service's sake has value. Service for the sake of sharing the gospel message and pointing people to God has great eternal value.

> **It's important that we continually share our testimonies of the Christian faith that leads us to serve.**

deflect it to the real source of light and grace and service in our lives.

In the short letter to his friend Philemon, Paul writes, "I pray that you may be active in sharing your faith, so that you will have a full understanding of every good thing we have in Christ" (v. 6 NIV). It seems to me that Paul is saying, "You will not have a *full* understanding of every good thing we have in Christ until you are active in sharing your faith."

As we lead our families in service before they know Christ, it's important that we continually share our testimonies of the Christian faith that leads us to serve. Once they become Christians themselves (the primary prayer we should all have for our families), one of the most important things we can do is train them to share their own personal testimonies of how they came to faith in Christ.

There are many tools and techniques today to help parents train their children (and themselves) in personal evangelism. Whichever of those we might choose, the two important disciplines are to make sure we know how to lead someone to faith in Christ and to see that we actually practice doing it. Surveys and statistics tell us that a majority of churchgoing Christians don't share their faith directly with anyone over the course of a year, and that means that most of our service to others is bringing them no eternal benefit. Let's be ready to give an account for the faith that motivates us to service and let our light attract people not to ourselves but to our Lord!

5. *Go on Mission Trips as a Family*

Jesus came and told his disciples, "I have been given complete authority in heaven and on earth. Therefore, go and make disciples of all the nations, baptizing them in the name of the Father and the Son and the Holy Spirit. Teach these new disciples to obey all the commands I have given you. And be sure of this: I am with you always, even to the end of the age."

Matthew 28:18–20

As I was looking through my email one day, I was surprised to see a message from my little niece. Once inside, I was a little disappointed to find not a personal note but one of those silly lists. This one was titled "Weird Things You Would Never Know." It included things like this:

- Elephants are the only animals that can't jump.
- Only one person in 2,000,000,000 will live to be 116 or older.
- Women blink nearly twice as much as men.
- It's physically impossible for you to lick your elbow.
- Our eyes are always the same size from birth, but our noses and ears never stop growing.
- The electric chair was invented by a dentist.
- *Typewriter* is the longest word that can be made using the letters on only one row of the keyboard.
- If Barbie were life-size, her measurements would be 39-23-33. She would stand seven feet, two inches tall.
- Almost everyone who reads this email will try to lick their elbow.

I have to admit, I was amused by this list as I read through it, and decided I would forgive my young niece for sending this particular junk email. But then the next weird thing on the list caught my attention in a special way.

It simply read, "'Go' is the shortest complete sentence in the English language."

Hmm . . . , I thought. *Interesting. I wonder if I would have been able to guess that answer on a quiz show*. In all of the English language, there's no quicker, simpler way to express a complete idea than with this little two-letter word.

And as I realized that the email list was right and that I couldn't think of a shorter sentence, I also realized that this silly little piece of trivia from a junk email was also a pretty big idea from the Bible. Time after time in the Bible when people have an experience with God (in the Old Testament) or meet Jesus (in the New Testament), they are then very shortly and simply commanded to *go* and be part of God's redemptive purposes, eventually inviting others to meet him too.

In Genesis 12:1 God says to Abraham, "Leave your country, your people and your father's household and *go* to the land I will show you" (NIV, emphasis added). In Exodus 3:10 God says to Moses, "So now, *go*. I am sending you to Pharaoh to bring my people the Israelites out of Egypt" (NIV, emphasis added). Jesus cast a legion of demons out of a man and then in Mark 5:19 told him, "*Go* home to your family and tell them how much the Lord has done for you, and how he has had mercy on you" (NIV, emphasis added). And then, of course, in Matthew 28 the risen Lord Jesus said to his disciples, including us, "All authority in heaven and on earth has been given to me. Therefore *go* and make disciples of all nations" (NIV, emphasis added).

One of the reasons "Go" can get by as a one-word sentence is that the subject of the sentence is assumed to be *you*. The sentence is really "You go," but all that's needed is the verb because it's a command whose subject is the person to whom the command is given. Throughout the Bible, the person who is to go is whoever has had a personal encounter with God. And in that case, that person is me. I can't treat that encounter like a junk email message and filter it out before it's acted upon. It's a personal message from my God. I'm to leave my place of comfort and go where others don't yet know Jesus.

Well, that silly little email list reminded me one more time that for Christians like me, "Go" is a complete sentence, a complete idea, and really a complete life purpose. How very much like God to pack such a big idea into such a small sentence.

One of the most memorable, powerful, and worthwhile experiences you can have with your family is to go on a mission trip together. It may take some work to find the right opportunity, one in which your entire family can find meaningful participation. But chances are in doing so you will experience all twelve practices mentioned in this book. You are likely to read together, eat together, play together, work together, worship together, and travel together. And yes, in the process you are likely to hurt together, change together, fight together, dream together, and serve together. Why not pray together now about the mission opportunity God might use to bond your family together in the way that Paul described in his letter to the Philippians:

> Every time I think of you, I give thanks to my God. I always pray for you, and I make my requests with a heart full of joy because you have been my partners in spreading the Good News about Christ from the time you first heard it until now. And I am sure that God, who began the good work within you, will continue his work until it is finally finished on that day when Christ Jesus comes back again.
>
> Philippians 1:3–6

> **One of the most memorable, powerful, and worthwhile experiences you can have with your family is to go on a mission trip together.**

Please *Do* Try This at Home

1. Lead your family in identifying a list of modern Christian heroes who demonstrate Christ-like character (love, humility, self-sacrifice) and whom you as a family will commit to both cheer and pray for. Include Christians from all arenas of life, including sports, entertainment, politics, and so on. Also include Christians you know personally such as your pastor, godly family members, perhaps people from your church who are living Christ-like examples in the marketplace. Whenever you see those heroes succeed in demonstrating servant leadership in their roles, cheer for them and find a way to encourage them.

2. Identify acts of secret service your family can do for others. Maybe it's raking their leaves or delivering surprise gifts that will encourage them. Maybe it's serving someone who's important to you without that person knowing why. Maybe your church has pathways of service you can tap into. As you serve together, talk openly about what right motives for service are.

3. Start planning a family mission trip, perhaps for next summer. Ask your church or mission board to help you find a project in which your whole family can provide meaningful, fulfilling service. Look for ways you can use that mission trip to do all twelve practices described in this book.

12

Preparing the Path

The Practice of Praying Together

Sometimes it seems like a long time ago, but I still remember what it was like to be a couple instead of a family. It was a time wonderfully blessed by things like uninterrupted conversations, a tidy house, weekend dates, and evening walks.

Yet as time passed, all those things seemed more and more like a prelude to something bigger. Our conversations turned more frequently to the topic of children. Our tidy house seemed to have an empty bedroom. Our weekend outings were often double dates with friends who needed babysitters. And before we knew it, our evening walks were not just times to dream about a family but times of recommended exercise for my expectant wife.

The night before our first son entered the world was the first of September, and it was one of those quiet evenings in late summer when our normal routine had become walking the streets of our neighborhood after dinner. As ready as I was to meet this little guy or girl, it was actually a week after Beth's due date, so my readiness was nothing compared to hers. Our doctor had told us that walking was about the best thing we could do to hasten the delivery, and by September 1 Beth was ready to consider mountain climbing and horseback riding as well.

That particular evening we had planned to eat dinner, take a long walk, and then come home to watch a video we had rented. In the middle of dinner, however, our house went dark. A quick check outside told us that the entire neighborhood was experiencing a power outage, the kind prompted by every house having its air conditioner turned on high at the same time. So we found a flashlight and started out into a night that was particularly silent and dark.

September 1 had always been a special, sentimental date for us, because that was the date of our first kiss. It was on our college campus while walking across the baseball field. We had always joked that our first kiss "came out of left field," which is the particular spot where we paused for that special event. Six years later I proposed marriage to Beth in that very spot. It was late December then rather than early September, and it was sleeting and freezing, but that's another romantic story for another time. The point is that evening walks and kissing and September 1 were all special to us. And on this last evening as a couple, we enjoyed all of them.

As we walked by flashlight and talked, we realized that this evening marked exactly ten years since that first kiss. We marveled at how quickly the time had passed and how time was likely to accelerate as soon as this baby joined us. It was a quiet, personal night. It was a night you only have once in your life.

Even on nights like that, though, a pregnant lady's feet swell. So we headed back to the house. Along the way we did something else we had grown accustomed to doing during this time of expectancy. We prayed for our child, for our family, and for our future. We prayed for his future wife or her future husband. We prayed for the friends who would mold our child's future. We prayed for health and safety. We prayed that one day Jesus Christ would be this child's Savior and Lord. We prayed for a day when we would all be together in heaven forever.

When we returned home the house was still dark. So much for the video plans. Instead, we lit a couple of candles and sat together on the bench of our used piano. I'm not a gifted composer or singer, but a few weeks earlier I had penned a little chorus based on Luke 2:52 that had simply come from my heart and became my prayer for my child. The simple lyrics went like this:

> May you increase in wisdom and stature, my child.
> May your favor with God and man grow.
> May you be like that little boy named Jesus,
> Who we're praying one day you'll come to know.

As I said, I'm not a gifted singer, but with just the two of us—and God and little unborn Caleb—there, it was OK. It was a song, but it was really more of a prayer. And so after I sang it a couple of times, we could just listen to it on the piano and let the prayer come from our hearts. We listened for a while and prayed and thought and prayed and talked and prayed. For us it was a silent, holy night.

That night we went to bed by flashlight, and every light, clock, and appliance in the house came back on at full volume early the next morning. It seemed to be an omen of life to come, because from that point forward it seemed that life has sped up dramatically. That day Caleb arrived and we began life as parents and not just a couple.

One boy, then two, then three. Different houses, different jobs, different churches. Work, school, sports, trips. Accomplishments, disappointments, times of celebration and sadness. Life just kind of took off after that special, silent night. But I will forever be grateful for that power outage on September 1. Because for me that silent night symbolizes the power that undergirds a winning family. It's a power that's there even by flashlight and even in the dark. It's the power that comes to parents by the practice of prayer.

In the theme song to the classic movie *Love Story*, the opening lyrics are "Where do I begin?" The song asks, "How do I describe the kind of love I've experienced and that I know will last forever?"

A family's story is a love story. And for the truly Christian family who wants God's love to be central in their story, the answer to "Where do I begin?" has to be prayer. I'm not really talking about the prayer you share as a family during devotional or worship times. Here I'm talking about the practice of prenatal, preschool, preadolescent, premarital, preemptive prayer. It's the practice of talking to God about our families in advance—long before we get to that stage of life.

> **For the truly Christian family who wants God's love to be central in their story, the answer to "Where do I begin?" has to be prayer.**

I don't know how to account for all the many blessings and privileges our family enjoys, or that other strong Christian families enjoy, except to know that God is their generous source. And I also know that the practice of inviting God into each stage of life long before we get there is somehow key to developing a happy, Christ-centered family.

Inviting God in by prayer is exactly what an unhappy wife named Hannah did.

> Hannah was in deep anguish, crying bitterly as she prayed to the Lord. And she made this vow: "O Lord Almighty, if you will look down upon my sorrow and answer my prayer and give me a son, then I will give him back to you. He will be yours for his entire lifetime, and as a sign that he has been dedicated to the Lord, his hair will never be cut."
>
> 1 Samuel 1:10–11

Though she had been barren for years, Hannah continued to pray passionately and continually for a family she couldn't yet see. If you look at the few verses that describe Hannah's life before her answered prayer, you don't find an ideal situation.

Hannah's husband, Elkanah, had another wife named Peninnah (strike one). Peninnah had children and Hannah didn't (strike two). Elkanah treated Hannah with some favoritism, and this no doubt fed the rivalry and jealousy between the two wives (strike three). Peninnah cruelly taunted Hannah about not having children. And how did Elkanah comfort her? First Samuel 1:8 says that Elkanah's attitude was basically, "Hey, baby, you have me! Aren't I better than ten kids?" Talk about a dysfunctional family situation!

Yet in spite of all this, God blessed Hannah with a special child, Samuel, who would be Israel's first great prophet as well as priest. Why? Well, certainly because God had sovereign plans for Hannah, for Samuel, and for Israel, but apparently also because Hannah prayed passionately in advance for her family.

Hannah was able to look ahead in faith and see a day when God would answer her prayer. So she kept praying, even when it hurt and even when God's answer did not come.

Have you discovered the benefits of praying in advance for your family? Here are some things we've discovered can help.

Helping Your Family Practice Praying in Advance as a Home Team

1. Prayer Is Best as Preparation, Not as Panic

A final word: Be strong with the Lord's mighty power. Put on all of God's armor so that you will be able to stand firm against all strategies and tricks of the Devil. For we are not fighting against people made of flesh and blood, but against the evil rulers and authorities of the unseen world, against those mighty powers of darkness who rule this world, and against wicked spirits in the heavenly realms.

Ephesians 6:10–12

Ephesians 5–6 gives us some of the Bible's most direct, practical advice for families. But after talking specifically about wives, husbands, children, parents, slaves, and masters, Paul closes his letter with this exhortation that seems to punctuate everything he's just written: Be prepared. Get ready for battle long before the battle arrives.

Why is praying in advance for your family so vital and so effective? Well, as with Hannah, praying in advance demonstrates faith. It shows that we believe God is able to deliver and that we trust him. It also shows that we understand how big God is. He can stand outside time and space, and yet he also stands inside our most intimate moments. He sees our future as well as our present and past. He sees the day of our children's death just as clearly as he sees the day of their conception. He's not surprised by anything. Trusting God with that kind of understanding pleases him because it demonstrates confidence in his character and his power.

As I played basketball in junior high and high school, I found myself prone to sprained ankles. So like many players on the team, I developed the habit of having my ankles taped before each game. Before one particularly big game, though, I was so excited and distracted that I neglected to have my ankles taped.

The first three quarters of that game were among the best I ever played as a high school athlete. With about a minute left in the third quarter, we led by eight points. I found out later that I had scored twenty-six points before I came crashing down on that untaped ankle. The pain was tremendous, but I wanted that win more than anything, and I insisted on going back in the game.

The problem was I couldn't even stand up. I spent the fourth quarter in the hospital emergency room getting my ankle x-rayed, and I didn't find out until returning home on crutches that we had gone on to lose that very important game.

The Bible says that standing up spiritually to the tough things of life has less to do with desire or ability than with preparation. Our most intimidating opponents—and those of our families—aren't as dangerous as the lack of preparation, which leaves us unprotected and vulnerable. Neither we nor our families will find the strength and protection to live for God in the moment of testing if we haven't stuck with the disciplines of prayer and relationship with him ahead of time.

Praying in advance for our families' needs is crucial to our future and the spiritual warfare we will all face, just as having our ankles taped is a crucial part of playing basketball. We just can't substitute last-minute hype for daily preparation. That's when we get hurt and can't stand at all.

David acknowledges in one of his prayers, "You saw me before I was born. Every day of my life was recorded in your book. Every moment was laid out before a single day had passed. How precious are your thoughts about me, O God! They are innumerable!" (Ps. 139:16–17). Paul writes to the Colossian church, "So we have continued praying for you ever since we first heard about you. We ask God to give you a complete understanding of what he wants to do in your lives, and we ask him to make you wise with spiritual wisdom" (Col. 1:9). And Jesus, in his passionate prayer before his betrayal and arrest, prays in advance for you and me when he says, "I am praying not only for these disciples but also for all who will ever believe in me because of their testimony" (John 17:20).

So pray in advance for your kids' friends and classmates. Pray for their enemies. Pray for their future spouses and for their future children. Pray for their teachers and their employers. Pray for their pastors and their spiritual leaders and mentors. Pray way on ahead into their lives. It's like building a road for them to walk on when they get there.

2. *Trust Your Family to God, Even during Life's Valleys*

Trust in the LORD with all your heart; do not depend on your own understanding. Seek his will in all you do, and he will direct your paths.

Proverbs 3:5–6

Paving the road of our families' future with prayer does not mean that we won't go through some valleys. In fact, trusting God through those valleys can be the times of richest growth and deepest relationship with him.

David acknowledges this special closeness to God in Psalm 23 when he writes, "Even when I walk through the dark valley of death, I will not be afraid, for you are close beside me. Your rod and your staff protect and comfort me" (vv. 4–5). In Proverbs 3:5–6 David's son Solomon, full of God's wisdom, urges us to trust God and not depend on our own understanding. Seeking God's will, Solomon assures us, will put us on a path of God's sure, trustworthy leadership.

I remember a time when a major decision was weighing on my mind and I really didn't know what to do. One of my options potentially had some pretty negative consequences. Another option seemed safe, but I couldn't get excited about it. Then there was the third option, the one I really wanted. But standing between me and that option were several huge obstacles, all of which were out of my control.

I had recently started praying about the decision. *Surely,* I thought, *God is powerful enough and interested enough in me to remove these obstacles that are frustrating me.* But day after day, then week after week, passed. And God wasn't delivering what I was asking for.

My thoughts were preoccupied with this decision as I drove through a gas station and then on to the automatic car wash I had earned with my fill-up.

"Put it in neutral, hands off the steering wheel." The bored-looking man's instructions didn't register with me. Lost in my own thoughts, I started driving forward toward the suds and spinning brushes.

"Hey . . . Hey! . . . HEY!" The man's voice had lost its monotone and was now cutting sternly into my private thoughts. "I said put it in neutral and keep your hands off the steering wheel!" It seemed to take all the restraint he could muster to keep from adding "you moron" to his impatient correction.

"Oh, I'm sorry. I was thinking about something else," I replied.

The man's weather-beaten face softened noticeably when he heard my apology, and he then tempered his impatience with a little car-wash wisdom: "It's automatic, son. You just bring the car up to this line. I do the rest."

As my car was slowly pulled from filthiness to cleanliness, I had a few minutes to compare that car wash to my prayers about the major decision I was facing. I wondered if God's apparent silence was his way of telling me I hadn't yet put my will in neutral and allowed him to steer my life to his will in this important matter. I was leaning on my own understanding. I wasn't really trusting him to guide me. I was merely asking him to give me what I wanted.

A couple of weeks later when God answered my prayer—with a fourth option that was better than anything I had thought of or imagined—I realized how important it was to put my will in neutral to seek God's guidance. And the car-wash man's words echoed again in my mind: "It's automatic, son. You just bring the car up to this line. I do the rest."

Sometimes it's even harder to trust God with our families than it is with our own concerns. Often we *can* help them through difficulty or solve their problems, and it's our loving intuition to do that whenever possible. But inevitably our families will outdistance our ability to fix or figure out their lives. But our prayers will always be able to reach them, and they will never outdistance the reach of our God, even when they walk through life's valleys.

3. Pray for the Whole Person

So Jesus grew both in height and in wisdom, and he was loved by God and by all who knew him.

Luke 2:52

In a way, we have very little information about Jesus's childhood. Yet in this one verse there's an amazing amount of insight into the way Jesus grew and the way we should want our families to grow. It says that Jesus grew physically ("height"), intellectually ("wisdom"), spiritually ("loved by

God"), and emotionally or socially ("loved by . . . all who knew him"). If we read different translations of the Bible, we can find different nuances of meaning to these four areas, but it's clear that they communicate a balanced, whole life. Jesus matured in all ways.

For over fifteen years now, Luke 2:52 has been my most consistent prayer for each of our children. I use it as a sort of outline for my prayers, one that guides me to pray in a balanced way for each of them as a whole person.

> **For over fifteen years now, Luke 2:52 has been my most consistent prayer for each of our children.**

First, I picture one of my sons in my mind and pray for his wisdom. Wherever he is in school, whatever subject he's struggling with, whatever lack of perspective or understanding he may be demonstrating at home or with his friends—I ask God to give him wisdom. Of course, biblical wisdom is more than intellectual ability. It's the God-given gift to see and understand things from God's perspective and to act accordingly. A life of wisdom is about more than a good report card.

Then I pray for that child's stature, and by that I also mean more than height. I pray that God will give my son continued health and safety and help him to grow naturally into physical maturity appropriate to his age. I pray that he'll be confident in his physical appearance and that he'll make good decisions that won't put him in physical danger. If he's been sick or had an injury of some sort, I pray for his healing and wellness. I pray that his physical condition will not limit him from fulfilling his life purposes.

Next I pray for that child's spiritual health, that he would be drawn close to God and be obedient to his leadership that day. (Of course, prior to the time each of our sons accepted Jesus as his personal Savior, I prayed that God would bring each one to the point of understanding his need for Christ and turning to him in repentance and faith.) I pray that God would give him a tender, teachable heart toward spiritual things and that his character would grow to be more like Christ. I pray that my son would have a love for God's Word and a deeper understanding of its truths and that he would apply what he knows in his life that day. I pray that he would find ways to make God smile that day.

And finally, I pray for that child's relationships, that he would be respected and liked for his integrity and compassion. I pray that he wouldn't fall into negative peer pressure, but that he would be a positive, Christian influence on his friends, his teachers, and others he might meet that day. I pray that God will continue to give him good friends and healthy friendships, and that when the time is right he'll bring the right young lady into his life. Sometimes I pray on ahead in his life, that he would have a healthy marriage, be a great husband and father, and have great relationships with his family.

Then I start on the second son and diligently pray through the same outline. The needs are different, not just because the boys are different ages but because they have different personalities and different kinds of challenges. In fact, the prayers are much more personal than what I've outlined here, because I need to pray about specific things like math quizzes, sore ankles, attitudes of rebellion, or mean classmates.

Of course, I pray for my wife and other family members as well, often with different Scriptures as guides. But when I'm praying for my children, who are still growing into maturity, I've found no more effective way to pray for the whole person than to continually pray through the balanced snapshot of Jesus's growth found in Luke 2:52. After all, my central prayer is that they would grow to be like Jesus.

4. Persist in Prayer

Then, teaching them more about prayer, he used this illustration: "Suppose you went to a friend's house at midnight, wanting to borrow three loaves of bread. You would say to him, 'A friend of mine has just arrived for a visit, and I have nothing for him to eat.' He would call out from his bedroom, 'Don't bother me. The door is locked for the night, and we are all in bed. I can't help you this time.' But I tell you this—though he won't do it as a friend, if you keep knocking long enough, he will get up and give you what you want so his reputation won't be damaged.

"And so I tell you, keep on asking, and you will be given what you ask for. Keep on looking, and you will find. Keep on knocking, and the door will be opened. For everyone who asks, receives. Everyone who seeks, finds. And the door is opened to everyone who knocks."

Luke 11:5–10

Sometimes the hardest thing about praying for people you love is to keep on praying when an answer is delayed. But Jesus repeatedly taught his disciples that persistence is one of the traits God values most in prayer. If it works on reluctant friends late at night or obstinate judges who don't even fear God (as in Luke 18:1–8), how much more will a loving God who delights in answering his children's prayers respond to their persistence and the faith it demonstrates?

> **Sometimes the hardest thing about praying for people you love is to keep on praying when an answer is delayed.**

Perhaps you know parents who have prayed for their children for years and years before God granted their request. Perhaps you're one of them. Jesus says, "Keep on asking. . . . Keep on looking. . . . Keep on knocking." Don't give up. Often it's only in hindsight that we can see why God delays an answer or says no.

It's always for our good if we love him and are pursuing his purposes.

My parents remind me from time to time about a couple of dating relationships I was in as an older teenager. They were so concerned that I was going to carelessly fall into a relationship with someone who did not have God as her top priority and that the rest of my life would be handicapped by that decision. I didn't know it at the time, but each time I headed out on a date with one of those girls, my mother faithfully prayed that God would protect me and guide me to the right girl. I don't think she knew with 100 percent certainty that girl couldn't be the one God had planned for me. But her 99 percent certainty kept her praying with persistence until God showed her she was right. As I reflect now on what is and what could have been, I'm so grateful for my parents' persistence in prayer on my behalf.

I recently came across a note in my Bible that I wrote when Beth and I had only one son, so it would have been in the first nineteen months of Caleb's life. It was a short list that was simply titled "What Caleb has taught me about prayer." Here's what was on that list:

- My son has unlimited access to me even when he doesn't see me.
- My son doesn't have to speak words for me to know when he needs something.
- Sometimes my son knows my tone, not my words.
- When my son looks at me attentively or smiles at me, I rejoice.
- When my son obeys me, I reward him, especially when he chooses obedience over what he really wants.
- My son's fear (respect) for me helps his obedience.
- My son's faith in me unleashes his potential.

- I don't always give my son what he wants, but I always want to give him what's best.

One of the benefits of parenthood is that we begin to see prayer more from God's perspective as a heavenly Father. And the more our own children ask us for things, the more we can understand why God answers prayer, or delays his answers, the way he does. It has given me greater encouragement and confidence to be persistent in prayer. God may want to build my trust in him, or he may see that my request isn't wise, or he may simply have something better in mind. Whatever the case, his answers have always, always been worth waiting for.

5. Celebrate God's Promises and Faithfulness

"You are blessed, because you believed that the Lord would do what he said."
　Mary responded,

"Oh, how I praise the Lord.
　How I rejoice in God my Savior!
For he took notice of his lowly servant girl,
　and now generation after generation will call me
　　blessed.
For he, the Mighty One, is holy,
　and he has done great things for me.
His mercy goes on from generation to generation,
　to all who fear him."

Luke 1:45–50

Both before God delivers and after he delivers, we have reason to celebrate his faithfulness. As we pray in advance for our families, we can rejoice in the many promises he has given us, confident that he always accomplishes his

215

word in his time. We can also rejoice when his promises are fulfilled and his blessings are realized in our lives.

When we discover a promise in God's Word that applies to our families, we should make it a matter of celebration—"Look at what God has said he will do! Look at what he says is true and available to us! Now we can pray in advance with great confidence, because God always honors his word." Mary's cousin Elizabeth declared that Mary was "blessed" even before Jesus was born. Why? Because Mary had already believed that the Lord would do what he said. The blessing comes from the moment of faith, not the moment of fulfillment.

> **When we discover a promise in God's Word that applies to our families, we should make it a matter of celebration—"Look at what God has said he will do!"**

We can also celebrate when God answers our prayers and blesses our families. Mary's celebration song in Luke 1 shows that she was already looking ahead to the days when future generations would be blessed by her child and would call her blessed for her God-given role.

When it comes to parenting, all of us are really lowly servants, chosen by God, as Mary described herself. Yet because God has given us the privilege of parenthood, we have the privilege of looking ahead to see how he might choose to bless future generations through our families. And we have the privilege of looking back to see how he has already demonstrated his faithfulness to us in our own lifetime.

So as we pray in advance for our families, and as we read, eat, play, work, worship, travel, hurt, change, fight, dream, and serve together, we have a great deal to celebrate. For he, the Mighty One, is holy, and he has done great things for us. His mercy goes on from generation to generation, to all who fear him.

Please *Do* Try This at Home

1. For each member of your family, draw out a life map on a single sheet of paper. Start at the left of the sheet with a dot that represents his or her birth and write his or her birth date under it. At the other end of the paper write a dot that symbolizes his or her death. In between, map out life events that will punctuate the average life of a person—grade school, high school, college, career, marriage, parenting, job changes, grandparenting, and so forth. Underneath each of the major seasons of life write down key relationships and challenges that family member may face.

   From these rough life maps, make your own prayer lists of key factors to pray about in the life of each family member. You may not take time to pray through the whole list each day (there are lots of daily needs to occupy your prayer time too!), but every so often use those prayer lists to pray in advance for the life needs of your family.

2. Sit down with your family (perhaps during a meal or family devotion time), and ask them to help you know how to pray for them in each of the areas of growth listed in Luke 2:52. In what ways do they need wisdom? What physical needs do they have? How can you pray for their spiritual lives these days? And what relationship needs could use your prayers? Use their input to guide your prayers not only for their future but also day by day as they grow toward Christ-likeness.

3. Plan an intentional celebration time for God's faithfulness and blessings in your family. It may be something fairly small, such as a good test grade, or something fairly large, such as a college graduation or promotion at work. Some gift shops sell special

plates you can use to honor a certain family member during mealtime that say something like "I am special today." Whatever method you use, plan celebrations that remind your family that God delivers on his promises and that he answers prayer.

Notes

1. Rick Warren, *The Purpose-Driven Life* (Grand Rapids: Zondervan, 2002), 277.

2. Robert Lewis, *Raising a Modern-Day Knight* (Wheaton: Tyndale House, 1997), 43, 63, 81.

3. Warren, *Purpose-Driven Life,* 23.

Nate Adams is the vice president of Mission Mobilization at the North American Mission Board of the Southern Baptist Convention. Adams also served for seventeen years at Christianity Today, Inc. An ordained minister, he has authored four books and numerous magazine articles in various Christian publications. He and his wife, Beth, have three sons and live in Duluth, Georgia.